MznLnx

Missing Links Exam Preps

Exam Prep for

Core Concepts of Management

Schermerhorn, 1st Edition

The MznLnx Exam Prep is your link from the texbook and lecture to your exams.
The MznLnx Exam Preps are unauthorized and comprehensive reviews of your textbooks.

All material provided by MznLnx and Rico Publications (c) 2010
Textbook publishers and textbook authors do not particpate in or contribute to these reviews.

MznLnx

Rico Publications

Exam Prep for Core Concepts of Management
1st Edition
Schermerhorn

Publisher: Raymond Houge	*Product Manager:* Dave Mason
Assistant Editor: Michael Rouger	*Editorial Assitant:* Rachel Guzmanji
Text and Cover Designer: Lisa Buckner	*Pedagogy:* Debra Long
Marketing Manager: Sara Swagger	*Cover Image:* Jim Reed/Getty Images
Project Manager, Editorial Production: Jerry Emerson	*Text and Cover Printer:* City Printing, Inc.
Art Director: Vernon Lowerui	*Compositor:* Media Mix, Inc.

(c) 2010 Rico Publications

ALL RIGHTS RESERVED. No part of this work covered by the copyright may be reproduced or used in any form or by an means--graphic, electronic, or mechanical, including photocopying, recording, taping, Web distribution, information storage, and retrieval systems, or in any other manner--without the written permission of the publisher.

For more information about our products, contact us at:
Dave.Mason@RicoPublications.com

For permission to use material from this text or product, submit a request online to:
Dave.Mason@RicoPublications.com

Printed in the United States
ISBN:

Contents

CHAPTER 1
MANAGEMENT TODAY — 1

CHAPTER 2
ENVIRONMENT, DIVERSITY, AND COMPETITIVE ADVANTAGE — 11

CHAPTER 3
GLOBALIZATION AND INTERNATIONAL MANAGEMENT — 20

CHAPTER 4
ETHICAL BEHAVIOR AND SOCIAL RESPONSIBILITY — 28

CHAPTER 5
PLANNING—TO SET DIRECTION — 34

CHAPTER 6
STRATEGIC MANAGEMENT AND ENTREPRENEURSHIP — 42

CHAPTER 7
CONTROLLING—TO ENSURE RESULTS — 52

CHAPTER 8
ORGANIZING—TO CREATE STRUCTURES — 60

CHAPTER 9
ORGANIZATIONAL CULTURE AND DESIGN — 65

CHAPTER 10
HUMAN RESOURCE SYSTEMS — 70

CHAPTER 11
LEADING—TO INSPIRE EFFORT — 82

CHAPTER 12
MOTIVATION AND JOB DESIGN — 85

CHAPTER 13
TEAMS AND TEAMWORK — 97

CHAPTER 14
COMMUNICATION AND INTERPERSONAL SKILLS — 101

CHAPTER 15
CHANGE LEADERSHIP AND STRESS — 106

ANSWER KEY — 114

TO THE STUDENT

COMPREHENSIVE

The *MznLnx* Exam Prep series is designed to help you pass your exams. Editors at MznLnx review your textbooks and then prepare these practice exams to help you master the textbook material. Unlike study guides, workbooks, and practice tests provided by the texbook publisher and textbook authors, *MznLnx* gives you **all** of the material in each chapter in exam form, not just samples, so you can be sure to nail your exam.

MECHANICAL

The MznLnx Exam Prep series creates exams that will help you learn the subject matter as well as test you on your understanding. Each question is designed to help you master the concept. Just working through the exams, you gain an understanding of the subject--its a simple mechanical process that produces success.

INTEGRATED STUDY GUIDE AND REVIEW

MznLnx is not just a set of exams designed to test you, its also a comprehensive review of the subject content. Each exam question is also a review of the concept, making sure that you will get the answer correct without having to go to other sources of material. You learn as you go! Its the easiest way to pass an exam.

HUMOR

Studying can be tedious and dry. MznLnx's instructional design includes moderate humor within the exam questions on occassion, to break the tedium and revitalize the brain

Chapter 1. MANAGEMENT TODAY

1. The term _____ collectively refers to all resources that determine the value and the competitiveness of an enterprise. As such, it includes as subsets the attributes that concur to building all financial statements as well as the balance sheet.
   a. AAAI
   b. A4e
   c. A Stake in the Outcome
   d. Intellectual capital

2. Procter is a surname, and may also refer to:

   - Bryan Waller Procter (pseud. Barry Cornwall), English poet
   - Goodwin Procter, American law firm
   - _____, consumer products multinational

   a. Procter ' Gamble
   b. Strict liability
   c. Downstream
   d. Master and Servant Acts

3. _____ is a strategic planning method used to evaluate the Strengths, Weaknesses, Opportunities, and Threats involved in a project or in a business venture. It involves specifying the objective of the business venture or project and identifying the internal and external factors that are favorable and unfavorable to achieving that objective. The technique is credited to Albert Humphrey, who led a convention at Stanford University in the 1960s and 1970s using data from Fortune 500 companies.
   a. Corporate image
   b. Marketing
   c. Market share
   d. SWOT analysis

4. _____ refers to metrics and measures of output from production processes, per unit of input. Labor _____, for example, is typically measured as a ratio of output per labor-hour, an input. _____ may be conceived of as a metrics of the technical or engineering efficiency of production.
   a. Productivity
   b. Value engineering
   c. Master production schedule
   d. Remanufacturing

5. _____ is any process of estimating or inferring how local policies, actions, or changes influences the state of the neighboring universe. It also can be defined, as an approach to problem solving, as viewing 'problems' as parts of an overall system, rather than reacting to present outcomes or events and potentially contributing to further development of the undesired issue or problem. _____ is a framework that is based on the belief that the component parts of a system can best be understood in the context of relationships with each other and with other systems, rather than in isolation.

   a. 1990 Clean Air Act
   b. 28-hour day
   c. Systems theory
   d. Systems thinking

6. _____ refers to the difference between the cost of materials purchased by a company plus the cost of the labor to assemble a product and the price at which the company sells the product. An example is the price of gasoline at the pump over the price of the oil in it. In national accounts used in macroeconomics, it refers to the contribution of the factors of production, i.e., land, labor, and capital goods, to raising the value of a product and corresponds to the incomes received by the owners of these factors.

   a. Minimum wage
   b. Rehn-Meidner Model
   c. Deregulation
   d. Value added

7. _____ can be considered to have three main components: quality control, quality assurance and quality improvement. _____ is focused not only on product quality, but also the means to achieve it. _____ therefore uses quality assurance and control of processes as well as products to achieve more consistent quality.

   a. 1990 Clean Air Act
   b. Total quality management
   c. 28-hour day
   d. Quality management

8. _____ is a business management strategy aimed at embedding awareness of quality in all organizational processes. _____ has been widely used in manufacturing, education, hospitals, call centers, government, and service industries, as well as NASA space and science programs.

As defined by the International Organization for Standardization (ISO):

> '_____ is a management approach for an organization, centered on quality, based on the participation of all its members and aiming at long-term success through customer satisfaction, and benefits to all members of the organization and to society.' ISO 8402:1994

One major aim is to reduce variation from every process so that greater consistency of effort is obtained. (Royse, D., Thyer, B., Padgett D., ' Logan T., 2006)

a. Total quality management
b. 28-hour day
c. 1990 Clean Air Act
d. Quality management

9. _____, widely known as F. W. Taylor, was an American mechanical engineer who sought to improve industrial efficiency. He is regarded as the father of scientific management, and was one of the first management consultants.

Taylor was one of the intellectual leaders of the Efficiency Movement and his ideas, broadly conceived, were highly influential in the Progressive Era.

a. Jonah Jacob Goldberg
b. Geoffrey Colvin
c. Douglas N. Daft
d. Frederick Winslow Taylor

10. The 'business case for _____', theorizes that in a global marketplace, a company that employs a diverse workforce (both men and women, people of many generations, people from ethnically and racially diverse backgrounds etc.) is better able to understand the demographics of the marketplace it serves and is thus better equipped to thrive in that marketplace than a company that has a more limited range of employee demographics.

An additional corollary suggests that a company that supports the _____ of its workforce can also improve employee satisfaction, productivity and retention.

a. Diversity
b. Virtual team
c. Trademark
d. Kanban

11. _____ has been described as the 'process of social influence in which one person can enlist the aid and support of others in the accomplishment of a common task' . A definition more inclusive of followers comes from Alan Keith of Genentech who said '_____ is ultimately about creating a way for people to contribute to making something extraordinary happen.'

_____ is one of the most salient aspects of the organizational context. However, defining _____ has been challenging.

a. Situational leadership
   b. 28-hour day
   c. 1990 Clean Air Act
   d. Leadership

12. _____ is a concept in ethics with several meanings. It is often used synonymously with such concepts as responsibility, answerability, enforcement, blameworthiness, liability and other terms associated with the expectation of account-giving. As an aspect of governance, it has been central to discussions related to problems in both the public and private (corporation) worlds.
   a. Usury
   b. A Stake in the Outcome
   c. Accountability
   d. A4e

13. _____ is a broad concept including proper prioritizing between career and ambition on one hand, compared with pleasure, leisure, family and spiritual development on the other.

As the separation between work and home life has diminished, this concept has become more relevant than ever before.

The expression was first used in the late 1970s to describe the balance between an individual's work and personal life.

   a. Quality of working life
   b. Work-life balance
   c. Workforce
   d. Division of labour

14. _____ occurs when expectant women are fired, not hired, or otherwise discriminated against due to their pregnancy or intention to become pregnant. Common forms of _____ include not being hired due to visible pregnancy or likelihood of becoming pregnant, being fired after informing an employer of one's pregnancy, being fired after maternity leave, and receiving a pay dock due to pregnancy. In the United States, since 1978, employers are legally bound to provide what insurance, leave pay, and additional support that would be bestowed upon any employee with medical leave or disability.
   a. 1990 Clean Air Act
   b. 28-hour day
   c. Pregnancy Discrimination
   d. 33 Strategies of War

Chapter 1. MANAGEMENT TODAY

15. _____ is an advertisement in which a particular product specifically mentions a competitor by name for the express purpose of showing why the competitor is inferior to the product naming it.

This should not be confused with parody advertisements, where a fictional product is being advertised for the purpose of poking fun at the particular advertisement, nor should it be confused with the use of a coined brand name for the purpose of comparing the product without actually naming an actual competitor. ('Wikipedia tastes better and is less filling than the Encyclopedia Galactica.')

In the 1980s, during what has been referred to as the cola wars, soft-drink manufacturer Pepsi ran a series of advertisements where people, caught on hidden camera, in a blind taste test, chose Pepsi over rival Coca-Cola.

a. 28-hour day
b. 33 Strategies of War
c. 1990 Clean Air Act
d. Comparative advertising

16. In economics, the term _____ refers to situations where the advancement of a qualified person within the hierarchy of an organization is stopped at a lower level because of some form of discrimination, most commonly sexism or racism, but since the term was coined, '_____' has also come to describe the limited advancement of the deaf, blind, disabled, aged and sexual minorities.It is an unofficial, invisible barrier that prevents women and minorities from advancing in businesses.

This situation is referred to as a 'ceiling' as there is a limitation blocking upward advancement, and 'glass' (transparent) because the limitation is not immediately apparent and is normally an unwritten and unofficial policy. This invisible barrier continues to exist, even though there are no explicit obstacles keeping minorities from acquiring advanced job positions - there are no advertisements that specifically say 'no minorities hired at this establishment', nor are there any formal orders that say 'minorities are not qualified' - but they do lie beneath the surface.

a. 33 Strategies of War
b. 1990 Clean Air Act
c. Glass ceiling
d. 28-hour day

Chapter 1. MANAGEMENT TODAY

17. _____ is an increasingly broadening term with which an organization, or other human system describes the combination of traditionally administrative personnel functions with acquisition and application of skills, knowledge and experience, Employee Relations and resource planning at various levels. The field draws upon concepts developed in Industrial/Organizational Psychology and System Theory. _____ has at least two related interpretations depending on context. The original usage derives from political economy and economics, where it was traditionally called labor, one of four factors of production although this perspective is changing as a function of new and ongoing research into more strategic approaches at national levels. This first usage is used more in terms of '_____ development', and can go beyond just organizations to the level of nations . The more traditional usage within corporations and businesses refers to the individuals within a firm or agency, and to the portion of the organization that deals with hiring, firing, training, and other personnel issues, typically referred to as `_____ management'.
    a. Bradford Factor
    b. Progressive discipline
    c. Human resources
    d. Human resource management

18. The _____ is the labour pool in employment. It is generally used to describe those working for a single company or industry, but can also apply to a geographic region like a city, country, state, etc. The term generally excludes the employers or management, and implies those involved in manual labour.
    a. Pink-collar worker
    b. Work-life balance
    c. Division of labour
    d. Workforce

19. _____ is a broad label that refers to any individuals or households that use goods and services generated within the economy. The concept of a _____ is used in different contexts, so that the usage and significance of the term may vary.

    Typically when business people and economists talk of _____s they are talking about person as _____, an aggregated commodity item with little individuality other than that expressed in the buy/not-buy decision.

    a. 28-hour day
    b. 33 Strategies of War
    c. 1990 Clean Air Act
    d. Consumer

20. The _____ was enacted in 1972 by the United States Congress. It established the United States Consumer Product Safety Commission as an independent agency of the United States federal government and defined its basic authority. The act gives CPSC the power to develop safety standards and pursue recalls for products that present unreasonable or substantial risks of injury or death to consumers.

a. 28-hour day
b. 33 Strategies of War
c. 1990 Clean Air Act
d. Consumer Product Safety Act

21. _____ is one of the managerial functions like planning, organizing, staffing and directing. It is an important function because it helps to check the errors and to take the corrective action so that deviation from standards are minimized and stated goals of the organization are achieved in desired manner.According to modern concepts, _____ is a foreseeing action whereas earlier concept of _____ was used only when errors were detected. _____ in management means setting standards, measuring actual performance and taking corrective action.
    a. Schedule of reinforcement
    b. Control
    c. Turnover
    d. Decision tree pruning

22. The _____ of 1967, Pub. L. No. 90-202, 81 Stat. 602 (Dec. 15, 1967), codified as Chapter 14 of Title 29 of the United States Code, 29 U.S.C. § 621 through 29 U.S.C. § 634 (ADEA), prohibits employment discrimination against persons 40 years of age or older in the United States). The law also sets standards for pensions and benefits provided by employers and requires that information about the needs of older workers be provided to the general public.
    a. Age Discrimination in Employment Act
    b. Extra time
    c. Undue hardship
    d. Unemployment and Farm Relief Act

23. _____ is a contract between two parties, one being the employer and the other being the employee. An employee may be defined as: 'A person in the service of another under any contract of hire, express or implied, oral or written, where the employer has the power or right to control and direct the employee in the material details of how the work is to be performed.' Black's Law Dictionary page 471 (5th ed. 1979.)
    a. Exit interview
    b. Employment rate
    c. Employment counsellor
    d. Employment

24. _____ is a term that was popularized by renowned psychologist David McClelland in 1961. However, it should be recognized that McClellend's thinking was strongly influenced by the pioneering work of Henry Murray who first identified underlying psychological human needs and motivational processes (1938.) It was Murray who set out a taxonomy of needs, including Achievement, Power and Affiliation - and placed these in the context of an integrated motivational model.

a. Two-factor theory
b. 1990 Clean Air Act
c. Need for Power
d. Need for Achievement

25. The _____ is the theory that the mass-news media have a large influence on audiences by their choice of what stories to consider newsworthy and how much prominence and space to give them. _____'s main postulate is salience transfer. Salience transfer is the ability of the mass media to transfer issues of importance from their mass media agendas to public agendas.
   a. A Stake in the Outcome
   b. A4e
   c. AAAI
   d. Agenda-setting theory

26. A _____ is the term given to a company that facilitates the learning of its members and continuously transforms itself. _____s develop as a result of the pressures facing modern organizations and enables them to remain competitive in the business environment. A _____ has five main features; systems thinking, personal mastery, mental models, shared vision and team learning.
   a. 1990 Clean Air Act
   b. Hoshin Kanri
   c. Learning organization
   d. Quality function deployment

27. _____ is a business management strategy, initially implemented by Motorola, that today enjoys widespread application in many sectors of industry.

_____ seeks to improve the quality of process outputs by identifying and removing the causes of defects (errors) and variation in manufacturing and business processes. It uses a set of quality management methods, including statistical methods, and creates a special infrastructure of people within the organization ('Black Belts' etc.)

   a. Theory of constraints
   b. Six Sigma
   c. Takt time
   d. Production line

Chapter 1. MANAGEMENT TODAY

28. _____ , often measured as an _____ Quotient (EQ), is a term that describes the ability, capacity, skill or (in the case of the trait _____ model) a self-perceived ability, to identify, assess, and manage the emotions of one's self, of others, and of groups. Different models have been proposed for the definition of _____ and disagreement exists as to how the term should be used. Despite these disagreements, which are often highly technical, the ability _____ and trait _____ models (but not the mixed models) are enjoying considerable support in the literature and have successful applications in many different domains.
   a. A4e
   b. A Stake in the Outcome
   c. AAAI
   d. Emotional intelligence

29. _____ was a writer, management consultant, and self-described 'social ecologist.' Widely considered to be 'the father of modern management,' his 39 books and countless scholarly and popular articles explored how humans are organized across all sectors of society--in business, government and the nonprofit world. His writings have predicted many of the major developments of the late twentieth century, including privatization and decentralization; the rise of Japan to economic world power; the decisive importance of marketing; and the emergence of the information society with its necessity of lifelong learning. In 1959, Drucker coined the term 'knowledge worker' and later in his life considered knowledge work productivity to be the next frontier of management.
   a. Jacques Al-Salawat Nasruddin Nasser
   b. Chrissie Hynde
   c. Debora L. Spar
   d. Peter Ferdinand Drucker

30. _____ is a term defined by the Oxford English Dictionary as an individual's 'course or progress through life '. It is usually considered to pertain to remunerative work (and sometimes also formal education.)

The etymology of the term is somewhat ironic in that it comes from the Latin word carrera, which means race .

   a. Spatial mismatch
   b. Nursing shortage
   c. Career planning
   d. Career

31. _____ comprises a range of practices used in an organisation to identify, create, represent, distribute and enable adoption of insights and experiences. Such insights and experiences comprise knowledge, either embodied in individuals or embedded in organisational processes or practice.

An established discipline since 1991 , _____ includes courses taught in the fields of business administration, information systems, management, and library and information sciences .

a. 33 Strategies of War
b. 28-hour day
c. 1990 Clean Air Act
d. Knowledge management

Chapter 2. ENVIRONMENT, DIVERSITY, AND COMPETITIVE ADVANTAGE

1. _____ was a writer, management consultant, and self-described 'social ecologist.' Widely considered to be 'the father of modern management,' his 39 books and countless scholarly and popular articles explored how humans are organized across all sectors of society--in business, government and the nonprofit world. His writings have predicted many of the major developments of the late twentieth century, including privatization and decentralization; the rise of Japan to economic world power; the decisive importance of marketing; and the emergence of the information society with its necessity of lifelong learning. In 1959, Drucker coined the term 'knowledge worker' and later in his life considered knowledge work productivity to be the next frontier of management.
   a. Debora L. Spar
   b. Chrissie Hynde
   c. Jacques Al-Salawat Nasruddin Nasser
   d. Peter Ferdinand Drucker

2. _____ in its literal sense is the process of transformation of local or regional phenomena into global ones. It can be described as a process by which the people of the world are unified into a single society and function together.

   This process is a combination of economic, technological, sociocultural and political forces.

   a. Cost Management
   b. Histogram
   c. Collaborative Planning, Forecasting and Replenishment
   d. Globalization

3. The term _____ collectively refers to all resources that determine the value and the competitiveness of an enterprise. As such, it includes as subsets the attributes that concur to building all financial statements as well as the balance sheet.
   a. AAAI
   b. A4e
   c. A Stake in the Outcome
   d. Intellectual capital

4. _____ comprises a range of practices used in an organisation to identify, create, represent, distribute and enable adoption of insights and experiences. Such insights and experiences comprise knowledge, either embodied in individuals or embedded in organisational processes or practice.

   An established discipline since 1991 , _____ includes courses taught in the fields of business administration, information systems, management, and library and information sciences .

Chapter 2. ENVIRONMENT, DIVERSITY, AND COMPETITIVE ADVANTAGE

   a. 33 Strategies of War
   b. 1990 Clean Air Act
   c. 28-hour day
   d. Knowledge management

5. _____ is, in very basic words, a position a firm occupies against its competitors.

According to Michael Porter, the three methods for creating a sustainable _____ are through:

1. Cost leadership

2. Differentiation

3. Focus (economics)

   a. Competitive advantage
   b. Theory Z
   c. 28-hour day
   d. 1990 Clean Air Act

6. The 'business case for _____', theorizes that in a global marketplace, a company that employs a diverse workforce (both men and women, people of many generations, people from ethnically and racially diverse backgrounds etc.) is better able to understand the demographics of the marketplace it serves and is thus better equipped to thrive in that marketplace than a company that has a more limited range of employee demographics.

An additional corollary suggests that a company that supports the _____ of its workforce can also improve employee satisfaction, productivity and retention.

   a. Kanban
   b. Trademark
   c. Virtual team
   d. Diversity

7. Organizational culture is not the same as _____. It is wider and deeper concepts, something that an organization 'is' rather than what it 'has' (according to Buchanan and Huczynski.)

_____ is the total sum of the values, customs, traditions and meanings that make a company unique.

a. Job analysis
b. Path-goal theory
c. Corporate culture
d. Work design

8. _____ occurs when expectant women are fired, not hired, or otherwise discriminated against due to their pregnancy or intention to become pregnant. Common forms of _____ include not being hired due to visible pregnancy or likelihood of becoming pregnant, being fired after informing an employer of one's pregnancy, being fired after maternity leave, and receiving a pay dock due to pregnancy. In the United States, since 1978, employers are legally bound to provide what insurance, leave pay, and additional support that would be bestowed upon any employee with medical leave or disability.
a. 1990 Clean Air Act
b. 33 Strategies of War
c. Pregnancy Discrimination
d. 28-hour day

9. In economics, the term _____ refers to situations where the advancement of a qualified person within the hierarchy of an organization is stopped at a lower level because of some form of discrimination, most commonly sexism or racism, but since the term was coined, '_____' has also come to describe the limited advancement of the deaf, blind, disabled, aged and sexual minorities. It is an unofficial, invisible barrier that prevents women and minorities from advancing in businesses.

This situation is referred to as a 'ceiling' as there is a limitation blocking upward advancement, and 'glass' (transparent) because the limitation is not immediately apparent and is normally an unwritten and unofficial policy. This invisible barrier continues to exist, even though there are no explicit obstacles keeping minorities from acquiring advanced job positions - there are no advertisements that specifically say 'no minorities hired at this establishment', nor are there any formal orders that say 'minorities are not qualified' - but they do lie beneath the surface.

a. Glass ceiling
b. 33 Strategies of War
c. 1990 Clean Air Act
d. 28-hour day

14 *Chapter 2. ENVIRONMENT, DIVERSITY, AND COMPETITIVE ADVANTAGE*

10. _____ is an increasingly broadening term with which an organization, or other human system describes the combination of traditionally administrative personnel functions with acquisition and application of skills, knowledge and experience, Employee Relations and resource planning at various levels. The field draws upon concepts developed in Industrial/Organizational Psychology and System Theory. _____ has at least two related interpretations depending on context. The original usage derives from political economy and economics, where it was traditionally called labor, one of four factors of production although this perspective is changing as a function of new and ongoing research into more strategic approaches at national levels. This first usage is used more in terms of '_____ development', and can go beyond just organizations to the level of nations. The more traditional usage within corporations and businesses refers to the individuals within a firm or agency, and to the portion of the organization that deals with hiring, firing, training, and other personnel issues, typically referred to as '_____ management'.

   a. Bradford Factor
   b. Progressive discipline
   c. Human resources
   d. Human resource management

11. _____ is an advertisement in which a particular product specifically mentions a competitor by name for the express purpose of showing why the competitor is inferior to the product naming it.

This should not be confused with parody advertisements, where a fictional product is being advertised for the purpose of poking fun at the particular advertisement, nor should it be confused with the use of a coined brand name for the purpose of comparing the product without actually naming an actual competitor. ('Wikipedia tastes better and is less filling than the Encyclopedia Galactica.')

In the 1980s, during what has been referred to as the cola wars, soft-drink manufacturer Pepsi ran a series of advertisements where people, caught on hidden camera, in a blind taste test, chose Pepsi over rival Coca-Cola.

   a. 28-hour day
   b. Comparative advertising
   c. 33 Strategies of War
   d. 1990 Clean Air Act

12. _____ has been described as the 'process of social influence in which one person can enlist the aid and support of others in the accomplishment of a common task'. A definition more inclusive of followers comes from Alan Keith of Genentech who said '_____ is ultimately about creating a way for people to contribute to making something extraordinary happen.'

_____ is one of the most salient aspects of the organizational context. However, defining _____ has been challenging.

Chapter 2. ENVIRONMENT, DIVERSITY, AND COMPETITIVE ADVANTAGE 15

   a. 1990 Clean Air Act
   b. Situational leadership
   c. 28-hour day
   d. Leadership

13. _____ is unwelcome harassment of a sexual nature, or based upon the receiving party's sex or gender. In some contexts or circumstances, _____ may be illegal. It includes a range of behavior from seemingly mild transgressions and annoyances to actual sexual abuse or sexual assault.

   a. 28-hour day
   b. 1990 Clean Air Act
   c. Hypernorms
   d. Sexual harassment

14.

The terms _____ and positive action refer to policies that take race, ethnicity, or gender into consideration in an attempt to promote equal opportunity. The focus of such policies ranges from employment and education to public contracting and health programs. The impetus towards _____ is twofold: to maximize diversity in all levels of society, along with its presumed benefits, and to redress perceived disadvantages due to overt, institutional, or involuntary discrimination.

   a. Abraham Harold Maslow
   b. Affirmative action
   c. Affiliation
   d. Adam Smith

15. _____ is the provision of service to customers before, during and after a purchase.

According to Turban et al. (2002), '_____ is a series of activities designed to enhance the level of customer satisfaction - that is, the feeling that a product or service has met the customer expectation.'

Its importance varies by product, industry and customer; defective or broken merchandise can be exchanged, often only with a receipt and within a specified time frame.

Chapter 2. ENVIRONMENT, DIVERSITY, AND COMPETITIVE ADVANTAGE

a. Service rate
b. 28-hour day
c. 1990 Clean Air Act
d. Customer service

16. _____ is an area of business concerned with the production of goods and services, and involves the responsibility of ensuring that business operations are efficient in terms of using as little resource as needed, and effective in terms of meeting customer requirements. It is concerned with managing the process that converts inputs (in the forms of materials, labour and energy) into outputs (in the form of goods and services.)

Operations traditionally refers to the production of goods and services separately, although the distinction between these two main types of operations is increasingly difficult to make as manufacturers tend to merge product and service offerings.

a. AAAI
b. Operations management
c. A Stake in the Outcome
d. A4e

17. _____ is a broad label that refers to any individuals or households that use goods and services generated within the economy. The concept of a _____ is used in different contexts, so that the usage and significance of the term may vary.

Typically when business people and economists talk of _____s they are talking about person as _____, an aggregated commodity item with little individuality other than that expressed in the buy/not-buy decision.

a. 28-hour day
b. 1990 Clean Air Act
c. 33 Strategies of War
d. Consumer

18. The _____ was enacted in 1972 by the United States Congress. It established the United States Consumer Product Safety Commission as an independent agency of the United States federal government and defined its basic authority. The act gives CPSC the power to develop safety standards and pursue recalls for products that present unreasonable or substantial risks of injury or death to consumers.

Chapter 2. ENVIRONMENT, DIVERSITY, AND COMPETITIVE ADVANTAGE

a. 28-hour day
b. Consumer Product Safety Act
c. 1990 Clean Air Act
d. 33 Strategies of War

19. In probability theory, a probability distribution is called _____ if its cumulative distribution function is _____. This is equivalent to saying that for random variables X with the distribution in question, Pr[X = a] = 0 for all real numbers a, i.e.: the probability that X attains the value a is zero, for any number a. If the distribution of X is _____ then X is called a _____ random variable.
   a. Decision tree pruning
   b. Pay Band
   c. Connectionist expert systems
   d. Continuous

20. _____ is a management process whereby delivery (customer valued) processes are constantly evaluated and improved in the light of their efficiency, effectiveness and flexibility.

Some see it as a meta process for most management systems (Business Process Management, Quality Management, Project Management). Deming saw it as part of the 'system' whereby feedback from the process and customer were evaluated against organisational goals.

   a. Critical Success Factor
   b. First-mover advantage
   c. Sole proprietorship
   d. Continuous Improvement Process

21. _____ can be considered to have three main components: quality control, quality assurance and quality improvement. _____ is focused not only on product quality, but also the means to achieve it. _____ therefore uses quality assurance and control of processes as well as products to achieve more consistent quality.
   a. Quality management
   b. 28-hour day
   c. Total quality management
   d. 1990 Clean Air Act

22. _____ is a business management strategy aimed at embedding awareness of quality in all organizational processes. _____ has been widely used in manufacturing, education, hospitals, call centers, government, and service industries, as well as NASA space and science programs.

Chapter 2. ENVIRONMENT, DIVERSITY, AND COMPETITIVE ADVANTAGE

As defined by the International Organization for Standardization (ISO):

'_____ is a management approach for an organization, centered on quality, based on the participation of all its members and aiming at long-term success through customer satisfaction, and benefits to all members of the organization and to society.' ISO 8402:1994

One major aim is to reduce variation from every process so that greater consistency of effort is obtained. (Royse, D., Thyer, B., Padgett D., ' Logan T., 2006)

  a. Total quality management
  b. Quality management
  c. 28-hour day
  d. 1990 Clean Air Act

23. _____ refers to the difference between the cost of materials purchased by a company plus the cost of the labor to assemble a product and the price at which the company sells the product. An example is the price of gasoline at the pump over the price of the oil in it. In national accounts used in macroeconomics, it refers to the contribution of the factors of production, i.e., land, labor, and capital goods, to raising the value of a product and corresponds to the incomes received by the owners of these factors.
  a. Rehn-Meidner Model
  b. Minimum wage
  c. Deregulation
  d. Value added

24. A _____ is a subset of the overall internal controls of a business covering the application of people, documents, technologies, and procedures by management accountants to solving business problems such as costing a product, service or a business-wide strategy. _____s are distinct from regular information systems in that they are used to analyze other information systems applied in operational activities in the organization. Academically, the term is commonly used to refer to the group of information management methods tied to the automation or support of human decision making, e.g. Decision Support Systems, Expert systems, and Executive information systems.
  a. 1990 Clean Air Act
  b. Strategic information system
  c. Management information system
  d. 28-hour day

25. A _____ is the term given to a company that facilitates the learning of its members and continuously transforms itself. _____s develop as a result of the pressures facing modern organizations and enables them to remain competitive in the business environment. A _____ has five main features; systems thinking, personal mastery, mental models, shared vision and team learning.

a. Learning organization
b. Hoshin Kanri
c. 1990 Clean Air Act
d. Quality function deployment

26. _____ is an area of knowledge within organizational theory that studies models and theories about the way an organization learns and adapts.

In Organizational development (OD), learning is a characteristic of an adaptive organization, i.e., an organization that is able to sense changes in signals from its environment (both internal and external) and adapt accordingly.

a. AAAI
b. A Stake in the Outcome
c. Organizational learning
d. A4e

Chapter 3. GLOBALIZATION AND INTERNATIONAL MANAGEMENT

1. _____ in its literal sense is the process of transformation of local or regional phenomena into global ones. It can be described as a process by which the people of the world are unified into a single society and function together.

This process is a combination of economic, technological, sociocultural and political forces.

   a. Collaborative Planning, Forecasting and Replenishment
   b. Cost Management
   c. Histogram
   d. Globalization

2. _____ is a type of trade policy that allows traders to act and transact without interference from government. Thus, the policy permits trading partners mutual gains from trade, with goods and services produced according to the theory of comparative advantage.

Under a _____ policy, prices are a reflection of true supply and demand, and are the sole determinant of resource allocation.

   a. Free Trade
   b. 33 Strategies of War
   c. 1990 Clean Air Act
   d. 28-hour day

3. _____ is a designated group of countries that have agreed to eliminate tariffs, quotas and preferences on most (if not all) goods and services traded between them. It can be considered the second stage of economic integration. Countries choose this kind of economic integration form if their economical structures are complementary.
   a. 1990 Clean Air Act
   b. 28-hour day
   c. 33 Strategies of War
   d. Free trade area

4. The _____ is a trilateral trade bloc in North America created by the governments of the United States, Canada, and Mexico. The agreement creating the trade bloc came into force on January 1, 1994. It superseded the Canada-United States Free Trade Agreement between the U.S. and Canada.
   a. Career portfolios
   b. Business war game
   c. North American Free Trade Agreement
   d. Trade union

Chapter 3. GLOBALIZATION AND INTERNATIONAL MANAGEMENT

5. _____ refers to the movement of cash into or out of a business or financial product. It is usually measured during a specified, finite period of time. Measurement of _____ can be used

   - to determine a project's rate of return or value. The time of _____s into and out of projects are used as inputs in financial models such as internal rate of return, and net present value.
   - to determine problems with a business's liquidity. Being profitable does not necessarily mean being liquid. A company can fail because of a shortage of cash, even while profitable.
   - as an alternate measure of a business's profits when it is believed that accrual accounting concepts do not represent economic realities. For example, a company may be notionally profitable but generating little operational cash (as may be the case for a company that barters its products rather than selling for cash.) In such a case, the company may be deriving additional operating cash by issuing shares evaluating default risk, re-investment requirements, etc.

   _____ is a generic term used differently depending on the context. It may be defined by users for their own purposes.

   a. Gross profit
   b. Gross profit margin
   c. Cash flow
   d. Sweat equity

6. A _____ or maquila is a factory that imports materials and equipment on a duty-free and tariff-free basis for assembly or manufacturing and then re-exports the assembled product, usually back to the originating country. A maquila is also referred to as a 'twin plant', or 'in-bond' industry. Nearly half a million Mexicans are employed in _____s.

   a. 1990 Clean Air Act
   b. Maquiladora
   c. 33 Strategies of War
   d. 28-hour day

7. _____ is an increasingly broadening term with which an organization, or other human system describes the combination of traditionally administrative personnel functions with acquisition and application of skills, knowledge and experience, Employee Relations and resource planning at various levels. The field draws upon concepts developed in Industrial/Organizational Psychology and System Theory. _____ has at least two related interpretations depending on context. The original usage derives from political economy and economics, where it was traditionally called labor, one of four factors of production although this perspective is changing as a function of new and ongoing research into more strategic approaches at national levels. This first usage is used more in terms of '_____ development', and can go beyond just organizations to the level of nations. The more traditional usage within corporations and businesses refers to the individuals within a firm or agency, and to the portion of the organization that deals with hiring, firing, training, and other personnel issues, typically referred to as '_____ management'.

Chapter 3. GLOBALIZATION AND INTERNATIONAL MANAGEMENT

a. Human resources
b. Bradford Factor
c. Progressive discipline
d. Human resource management

8. _____ has been described as the 'process of social influence in which one person can enlist the aid and support of others in the accomplishment of a common task'. A definition more inclusive of followers comes from Alan Keith of Genentech who said '_____ is ultimately about creating a way for people to contribute to making something extraordinary happen.'

_____ is one of the most salient aspects of the organizational context. However, defining _____ has been challenging.

a. 28-hour day
b. 1990 Clean Air Act
c. Leadership
d. Situational leadership

9. _____ is exchange of capital, goods, and services across international borders or territories. In most countries, it represents a significant share of gross domestic product (GDP.) While _____ has been present throughout much of history, its economic, social, and political importance has been on the rise in recent centuries.

a. AAAI
b. A4e
c. A Stake in the Outcome
d. International trade

10. _____ refers to the methods of practicing and using another person's business philosophy. The franchisor grants the independent operator the right to distribute its products, techniques, and trademarks for a percentage of gross monthly sales and a royalty fee. Various tangibles and intangibles such as national or international advertising, training, and other support services are commonly made available by the franchisor.

a. 28-hour day
b. 1990 Clean Air Act
c. ServiceMaster
d. Franchising

Chapter 3. GLOBALIZATION AND INTERNATIONAL MANAGEMENT

11. _____ is a term used to describe practice of sourcing from the global market for goods and services across geopolitical boundaries. _____ often aims to exploit global efficiencies in the delivery of a product or service. These efficiencies include low cost skilled labor, low cost raw material and other economic factors like tax breaks and low trade tariffs.
   a. Global sourcing
   b. 1990 Clean Air Act
   c. Purchasing process
   d. Purchase requisition

12. A _____ is an entity formed between two or more parties to undertake economic activity together. The parties agree to create a new entity by both contributing equity, and they then share in the revenues, expenses, and control of the enterprise. The venture can be for one specific project only, or a continuing business relationship such as the Fuji Xerox _____.
   a. Meritor Savings Bank v. Vinson
   b. Joint venture
   c. Civil Rights Act of 1991
   d. Patent

13. In business, the term word _____ refers to a number of procurement practices, aimed at finding, evaluating and engaging suppliers of goods and services:

   - Global _____, a procurement strategy aimed at exploiting global efficiencies in production
   - Strategic _____, a component of supply chain management, for improving and re-evaluating purchasing activities
   - _____, the identification of job candidates through proactive recruiting technique
   - Co-_____, a type of auditing service
   - Low-cost country _____, a procurement strategy for acquiring materials from countries with lower labour and production costs in order to cut operating expenses
   - Corporate _____, a supply chain, purchasing/procurement, and inventory function
   - Second-tier _____, a practice of rewarding suppliers for attempting to achieve minority-owned business spending goals of their customer
   - Netsourcing, a practice of utilizing an established group of businesses, individuals, or hardware ' software applications to streamline or initiate procurement practices by tapping in to and working through a third party provider
   - Inverted _____, a price volatility reduction strategy usually conducted by procurement or supply-chain person by which the value of an organization's waste-stream is maximized by actively seeking out the highest price possible from a range of potential buyers exploiting price trends and other market factors
   - Multisourcing, a strategy that treats a given function, such as IT, as a portfolio of activities, some of which should be outsourced and others of which should be performed by internal staff.
   - Crowdsourcing, using an undefined, generally large group of people or community in the form of an open call to perform a task

Chapter 3. GLOBALIZATION AND INTERNATIONAL MANAGEMENT

In journalism, it can also refer to:

- Journalism _____, the practice of identifying a person or publication that gives information
- Single _____, the reuse of content in publishing

In computing, it can refer to:

- Open-_____, the act of releasing previously proprietary software under an open source/free software license
- Power _____ equipment, network devices that will provide power in a Power over Ethernet (PoE) setup

  a. Cost Management
  b. Reinforcement
  c. Continuous
  d. Sourcing

14. An _____ is a person who has possession of an enterprise and assumes significant accountability for the inherent risks and the outcome. It is an ambitious leader who combines land, labor, and capital to create and market new goods or services. The term is a loanword from French and was first defined by the Irish economist Richard Cantillon.
  a. A Stake in the Outcome
  b. AAAI
  c. A4e
  d. Entrepreneur

15. A _____, in business matters, is an entity that is controlled by a bigger and more powerful entity. The controlled entity is called a company, corporation, or limited liability company and in some cases can be a government or state-owned enterprise, and the controlling entity is called its parent (or the parent company.) The reason for this distinction is that a lone company cannot be a _____ of any organization; only an entity representing a legal fiction as a separate entity can be a _____.
  a. 1990 Clean Air Act
  b. 28-hour day
  c. 33 Strategies of War
  d. Subsidiary

16. A _____ or transnational corporation is a corporation or enterprise that manages production or delivers services in more than one country. It can also be referred to as an international corporation.

Chapter 3. GLOBALIZATION AND INTERNATIONAL MANAGEMENT

The first modern _____ is generally thought to be the Dutch East India Company, established in 1602.

a. Small and medium enterprises
b. Financial Accounting Standards Board
c. Command center
d. Multinational corporation

17. The 'business case for _____', theorizes that in a global marketplace, a company that employs a diverse workforce (both men and women, people of many generations, people from ethnically and racially diverse backgrounds etc.) is better able to understand the demographics of the marketplace it serves and is thus better equipped to thrive in that marketplace than a company that has a more limited range of employee demographics.

An additional corollary suggests that a company that supports the _____ of its workforce can also improve employee satisfaction, productivity and retention.

a. Virtual team
b. Diversity
c. Trademark
d. Kanban

18. The _____ of 1977 (15 U.S.C. §§ 78dd-1, et seq.) is a United States federal law known primarily for two of its main provisions, one that addresses accounting transparency requirements under the Securities Exchange Act of 1934 and another concerning bribery of foreign officials.

a. Meritor Savings Bank v. Vinson
b. Social Security Act of 1965
c. Limited liability
d. Foreign Corrupt Practices Act

19. _____ is a broad philosophy and social movement regarding concerns for environmental conservation and improvement of the environment. _____ and environmental concerns may be represented with the color green.

_____ can also be defined as a social movement that seeks to influence the political process by lobbying, activism, and education in order to protect natural resources and ecosystems.

Chapter 3. GLOBALIZATION AND INTERNATIONAL MANAGEMENT

a. A Stake in the Outcome
b. Industrial ecology
c. Environmentalism
d. A4e

20. A _____ is a working environment with conditions that are considered by many people of industrialized nations to be difficult or dangerous, usually where the workers have few opportunities to address their situation. This can include exposure to harmful materials, hazardous situations, extreme temperatures, or abuse from employers. _____ workers often work long hours for little pay, regardless of any laws mandating overtime pay or a minimum wage.

a. Rate of return
b. Continuous
c. Complement
d. Sweatshop

21. _____ is an idea in the field of Organizational studies and management which describes the psychology, attitudes, experiences, beliefs and Values (personal and cultural values) of an organization. It has been defined as 'the specific collection of values and norms that are shared by people and groups in an organization and that control the way they interact with each other and with stakeholders outside the organization.'

This definition continues to explain organizational values also known as 'beliefs and ideas about what kinds of goals members of an organization should pursue and ideas about the appropriate kinds or standards of behavior organizational members should use to achieve these goals. From organizational values develop organizational norms, guidelines or expectations that prescribe appropriate kinds of behavior by employees in particular situations and control the behavior of organizational members towards one another.'

_____ is not the same as corporate culture.

a. Union shop
b. Organizational effectiveness
c. Organizational development
d. Organizational culture

22. _____ is a broad label that refers to any individuals or households that use goods and services generated within the economy. The concept of a _____ is used in different contexts, so that the usage and significance of the term may vary.

Typically when business people and economists talk of _____s they are talking about person as _____, an aggregated commodity item with little individuality other than that expressed in the buy/not-buy decision.

Chapter 3. GLOBALIZATION AND INTERNATIONAL MANAGEMENT

a. Consumer
b. 1990 Clean Air Act
c. 28-hour day
d. 33 Strategies of War

23. The _____ was enacted in 1972 by the United States Congress. It established the United States Consumer Product Safety Commission as an independent agency of the United States federal government and defined its basic authority. The act gives CPSC the power to develop safety standards and pursue recalls for products that present unreasonable or substantial risks of injury or death to consumers.

a. 1990 Clean Air Act
b. 28-hour day
c. 33 Strategies of War
d. Consumer Product Safety Act

24. The term _____ was introduced by anthropologist Edward T. Hall in 1966 to describe set measurable distances between people as they interact. The effects of _____, according to Hall, can be summarized by the following loose rule:

According to Jonathon Tabor distance-spacing theories based on the early animal-like human of German zoologist Heini Hediger, as found in his 1955 book Studies of the Behavior of Captive Animals in Zoos and Circuses. Hediger, in animals, had distinguished between flight distance , critical distance (attack boundary), personal distance (distance separating members of non-contact species, as a pair of swans), and social distance (intraspecies communication distance.)

a. 28-hour day
b. 1990 Clean Air Act
c. 33 Strategies of War
d. Proxemics

Chapter 4. ETHICAL BEHAVIOR AND SOCIAL RESPONSIBILITY

1. _____ is an advertisement in which a particular product specifically mentions a competitor by name for the express purpose of showing why the competitor is inferior to the product naming it.

This should not be confused with parody advertisements, where a fictional product is being advertised for the purpose of poking fun at the particular advertisement, nor should it be confused with the use of a coined brand name for the purpose of comparing the product without actually naming an actual competitor. ('Wikipedia tastes better and is less filling than the Encyclopedia Galactica.')

In the 1980s, during what has been referred to as the cola wars, soft-drink manufacturer Pepsi ran a series of advertisements where people, caught on hidden camera, in a blind taste test, chose Pepsi over rival Coca-Cola.

   a. 28-hour day
   b. 33 Strategies of War
   c. 1990 Clean Air Act
   d. Comparative advertising

2. A _____ occurs when an individual or organization (such as a policeman, lawyer, insurance adjuster, politician, engineer, executive, director of a corporation, medical research scientist, physician, writer, editor, or any other entrusted individual or organization) has an interest that might compromise their actions. The presence of a _____ is independent from the execution of impropriety.

In the legal profession, the duty of loyalty owed to a client prohibits an attorney (or a law firm) from representing any other party with interests adverse to those of a current client.

   a. 1990 Clean Air Act
   b. Global Corruption Report
   c. Conflict of interest
   d. 28-hour day

3. _____ is an increasingly broadening term with which an organization, or other human system describes the combination of traditionally administrative personnel functions with acquisition and application of skills, knowledge and experience, Employee Relations and resource planning at various levels. The field draws upon concepts developed in Industrial/Organizational Psychology and System Theory. _____ has at least two related interpretations depending on context. The original usage derives from political economy and economics, where it was traditionally called labor, one of four factors of production although this perspective is changing as a function of new and ongoing research into more strategic approaches at national levels. This first usage is used more in terms of '_____ development', and can go beyond just organizations to the level of nations . The more traditional usage within corporations and businesses refers to the individuals within a firm or agency, and to the portion of the organization that deals with hiring, firing, training, and other personnel issues, typically referred to as `_____ management'.

Chapter 4. ETHICAL BEHAVIOR AND SOCIAL RESPONSIBILITY

   a. Human resource management
   b. Progressive discipline
   c. Human resources
   d. Bradford Factor

4. _____ has been described as the 'process of social influence in which one person can enlist the aid and support of others in the accomplishment of a common task' . A definition more inclusive of followers comes from Alan Keith of Genentech who said '_____ is ultimately about creating a way for people to contribute to making something extraordinary happen.'

_____ is one of the most salient aspects of the organizational context. However, defining _____ has been challenging.

   a. 28-hour day
   b. Leadership
   c. Situational leadership
   d. 1990 Clean Air Act

5. _____ is unwelcome harassment of a sexual nature, or based upon the receiving party's sex or gender. In some contexts or circumstances, _____ may be illegal. It includes a range of behavior from seemingly mild transgressions and annoyances to actual sexual abuse or sexual assault.
   a. Sexual harassment
   b. Hypernorms
   c. 28-hour day
   d. 1990 Clean Air Act

6. _____ is a concept in ethics with several meanings. It is often used synonymously with such concepts as responsibility, answerability, enforcement, blameworthiness, liability and other terms associated with the expectation of account-giving. As an aspect of governance, it has been central to discussions related to problems in both the public and private (corporation) worlds.
   a. A4e
   b. Usury
   c. A Stake in the Outcome
   d. Accountability

Chapter 4. ETHICAL BEHAVIOR AND SOCIAL RESPONSIBILITY

7. _____ is a form of corporate self-regulation integrated into a business model. Ideally, _____ policy would function as a built-in, self-regulating mechanism whereby business would monitor and ensure their adherence to law, ethical standards, and international norms. Business would embrace responsibility for the impact of their activities on the environment, consumers, employees, communities, stakeholders and all other members of the public sphere.
   a. 28-hour day
   b. 33 Strategies of War
   c. Corporate social responsibility
   d. 1990 Clean Air Act

8. The general definition of an _____ is an evaluation of a person, organization, system, process, project or product. _____s are performed to ascertain the validity and reliability of information; also to provide an assessment of a system's internal control. The goal of an _____ is to express an opinion on the person / organization/system (etc) in question, under evaluation based on work done on a test basis.
   a. A Stake in the Outcome
   b. Audit committee
   c. Internal control
   d. Audit

9. _____ is a broad label that refers to any individuals or households that use goods and services generated within the economy. The concept of a _____ is used in different contexts, so that the usage and significance of the term may vary.

Typically when business people and economists talk of _____s they are talking about person as _____, an aggregated commodity item with little individuality other than that expressed in the buy/not-buy decision.

   a. Consumer
   b. 33 Strategies of War
   c. 28-hour day
   d. 1990 Clean Air Act

10. The _____ was enacted in 1972 by the United States Congress. It established the United States Consumer Product Safety Commission as an independent agency of the United States federal government and defined its basic authority. The act gives CPSC the power to develop safety standards and pursue recalls for products that present unreasonable or substantial risks of injury or death to consumers.

Chapter 4. ETHICAL BEHAVIOR AND SOCIAL RESPONSIBILITY

   a. 28-hour day
   b. Consumer Product Safety Act
   c. 1990 Clean Air Act
   d. 33 Strategies of War

11. _____ is one of the managerial functions like planning, organizing, staffing and directing. It is an important function because it helps to check the errors and to take the corrective action so that deviation from standards are minimized and stated goals of the organization are achieved in desired manner. According to modern concepts, _____ is a foreseeing action whereas earlier concept of _____ was used only when errors were detected. _____ in management means setting standards, measuring actual performance and taking corrective action.
   a. Control
   b. Schedule of reinforcement
   c. Turnover
   d. Decision tree pruning

12. _____ is a contract between two parties, one being the employer and the other being the employee. An employee may be defined as: 'A person in the service of another under any contract of hire, express or implied, oral or written, where the employer has the power or right to control and direct the employee in the material details of how the work is to be performed.' Black's Law Dictionary page 471 (5th ed. 1979.)
   a. Exit interview
   b. Employment counsellor
   c. Employment rate
   d. Employment

13. The term _____ was created by President Lyndon B. Johnson when he signed Executive Order 11246 on September 24, 1965, created to prohibit federal contractors from discriminating against employees on the basis of race, sex, creed, religion, color, or national origin. In more recent times, most employers have also added sexual orientation to the list of non-discrimination.

The Executive Order also required contractors to implement affirmative action plans to increase the participation of minorities and women in the workplace.

   a. AAAI
   b. A4e
   c. A Stake in the Outcome
   d. Equal Employment Opportunity

Chapter 4. ETHICAL BEHAVIOR AND SOCIAL RESPONSIBILITY

14. _____ is a cross-disciplinary area concerned with protecting the safety, health and welfare of people engaged in work or employment. The goal of all _____ programs is to foster a work free safe environment. As a secondary effect, it may also protect co-workers, family members, employers, customers, suppliers, nearby communities, and other members of the public who are impacted by the workplace environment.
   a. Occupational Safety and Health
   b. A Stake in the Outcome
   c. AAAI
   d. A4e

15. The _____ is the primary federal law which governs occupational health and safety in the private sector and federal government in the United States. It was enacted by Congress in 1970 and was signed by President Richard Nixon on December 29, 1970. Its main goal is to ensure that employers provide employees with an environment free from recognized hazards, such as exposure to toxic chemicals, excessive noise levels, mechanical dangers, heat or cold stress, or unsanitary conditions.
   a. Unemployment and Farm Relief Act
   b. United States Department of Justice
   c. Unemployment Action Center
   d. Occupational Safety and Health Act

16. Procter is a surname, and may also refer to:

   - Bryan Waller Procter (pseud. Barry Cornwall), English poet
   - Goodwin Procter, American law firm
   - _____, consumer products multinational

   a. Downstream
   b. Master and Servant Acts
   c. Strict liability
   d. Procter ' Gamble

17. The _____ of 2002 (Pub.L. 107-204, 116 Stat. 745, enacted July 30, 2002), also known as the Public Company Accounting Reform and Investor Protection Act of 2002 and commonly called Sarbanes-Oxley, Sarbox or SOX, is a United States federal law enacted on July 30, 2002, as a reaction to a number of major corporate and accounting scandals including those affecting Enron, Tyco International, Adelphia, Peregrine Systems and WorldCom.

Chapter 4. ETHICAL BEHAVIOR AND SOCIAL RESPONSIBILITY

a. Sarbanes-Oxley Act
b. Letter of credit
c. Sarbanes-Oxley Act of 2002
d. Fair Labor Standards Act

18. The U.S. _____ is an independent agency of the United States government which holds primary responsibility for enforcing the federal securities laws and regulating the securities industry, the nation's stock and options exchanges, and other electronic securities markets. The SEC was created by section 4 of the Securities Exchange Act of 1934 (now codified as 15 U.S.C. Â§ 78d and commonly referred to as the 1934 Act.)

a. 33 Strategies of War
b. 1990 Clean Air Act
c. 28-hour day
d. Securities and Exchange Commission

19. _____ is a broad philosophy and social movement regarding concerns for environmental conservation and improvement of the environment. _____ and environmental concerns may be represented with the color green.

_____ can also be defined as a social movement that seeks to influence the political process by lobbying, activism, and education in order to protect natural resources and ecosystems.

a. A4e
b. A Stake in the Outcome
c. Industrial ecology
d. Environmentalism

Chapter 5. PLANNING—TO SET DIRECTION

1. _____ is an increasingly broadening term with which an organization, or other human system describes the combination of traditionally administrative personnel functions with acquisition and application of skills, knowledge and experience, Employee Relations and resource planning at various levels. The field draws upon concepts developed in Industrial/Organizational Psychology and System Theory. _____ has at least two related interpretations depending on context. The original usage derives from political economy and economics, where it was traditionally called labor, one of four factors of production although this perspective is changing as a function of new and ongoing research into more strategic approaches at national levels. This first usage is used more in terms of '_____ development', and can go beyond just organizations to the level of nations . The more traditional usage within corporations and businesses refers to the individuals within a firm or agency, and to the portion of the organization that deals with hiring, firing, training, and other personnel issues, typically referred to as `_____ management'.

   a. Human resource management
   b. Progressive discipline
   c. Bradford Factor
   d. Human resources

2. _____ can be considered to have three main components: quality control, quality assurance and quality improvement. _____ is focused not only on product quality, but also the means to achieve it. _____ therefore uses quality assurance and control of processes as well as products to achieve more consistent quality.

   a. 1990 Clean Air Act
   b. 28-hour day
   c. Total quality management
   d. Quality management

3. _____ is a business management strategy aimed at embedding awareness of quality in all organizational processes. _____ has been widely used in manufacturing, education, hospitals, call centers, government, and service industries, as well as NASA space and science programs.

   As defined by the International Organization for Standardization (ISO):

   '_____ is a management approach for an organization, centered on quality, based on the participation of all its members and aiming at long-term success through customer satisfaction, and benefits to all members of the organization and to society.' ISO 8402:1994

   One major aim is to reduce variation from every process so that greater consistency of effort is obtained. (Royse, D., Thyer, B., Padgett D., ' Logan T., 2006)

   a. Quality management
   b. Total quality management
   c. 28-hour day
   d. 1990 Clean Air Act

Chapter 5. PLANNING—TO SET DIRECTION

4. _____ is an advertisement in which a particular product specifically mentions a competitor by name for the express purpose of showing why the competitor is inferior to the product naming it.

This should not be confused with parody advertisements, where a fictional product is being advertised for the purpose of poking fun at the particular advertisement, nor should it be confused with the use of a coined brand name for the purpose of comparing the product without actually naming an actual competitor. ('Wikipedia tastes better and is less filling than the Encyclopedia Galactica.')

In the 1980s, during what has been referred to as the cola wars, soft-drink manufacturer Pepsi ran a series of advertisements where people, caught on hidden camera, in a blind taste test, chose Pepsi over rival Coca-Cola.

   a. 28-hour day
   b. 1990 Clean Air Act
   c. 33 Strategies of War
   d. Comparative advertising

5. _____ refers to a range of skills, tools, and techniques used to manage time when accomplishing specific tasks, projects and goals. This set encompass a wide scope of activities, and these include planning, allocating, setting goals, delegation, analysis of time spent, monitoring, organizing, scheduling, and prioritizing. Initially _____ referred to just business or work activities, but eventually the term broadened to include personal activities also.
   a. Voice of the customer
   b. Time management
   c. Cash cow
   d. Formula for Change

6. The _____ is a monograph published by Frederick Winslow Taylor in 1911. This influential monograph is the basis of modern organization and decision theory and has motivated administrators and students of managerial technique. Taylor was an American mechanical engineer and a management consultant in his later years.
   a. 1990 Clean Air Act
   b. 28-hour day
   c. 33 Strategies of War
   d. Principles of Scientific Management

7. _____ is a theory of management that analyzes and synthesizes workflows, with the objective of improving labour productivity. The core ideas of the theory were developed by Frederick Winslow Taylor in the 1880s and 1890s, and were first published in his monographs, Shop Management and The Principles of _____ Taylor believed that decisions based upon tradition and rules of thumb should be replaced by precise procedures developed after careful study of an individual at work.

Chapter 5. PLANNING—TO SET DIRECTION

a. Master production schedule
b. Scientific Management
c. Value engineering
d. Capacity planning

8. _____ are a set of documents that describe an organization's policies for operation and the procedures necessary to fulfill the policies. They are often initiated because of some external requirement, such as environmental compliance or other governmental regulations, such as the American Sarbanes-Oxley Act requiring full openness in accounting practices. The easiest way to start writing _____ is to interview the users of the _____ and create a flow chart or task map or work flow of the process from start to finish.

a. Group booking
b. Customer retention
c. Horizontal integration
d. Policies and procedures

9. _____ refers to the movement of cash into or out of a business or financial product. It is usually measured during a specified, finite period of time. Measurement of _____ can be used

- to determine a project's rate of return or value. The time of _____s into and out of projects are used as inputs in financial models such as internal rate of return, and net present value.
- to determine problems with a business's liquidity. Being profitable does not necessarily mean being liquid. A company can fail because of a shortage of cash, even while profitable.
- as an alternate measure of a business's profits when it is believed that accrual accounting concepts do not represent economic realities. For example, a company may be notionally profitable but generating little operational cash (as may be the case for a company that barters its products rather than selling for cash.) In such a case, the company may be deriving additional operating cash by issuing shares evaluating default risk, re-investment requirements, etc.

_____ is a generic term used differently depending on the context. It may be defined by users for their own purposes.

a. Gross profit
b. Cash flow
c. Sweat equity
d. Gross profit margin

10. _____ generally refers to a list of all planned expenses and revenues. It is a plan for saving and spending. A _____ is an important concept in microeconomics, which uses a _____ line to illustrate the trade-offs between two or more goods.

Chapter 5. PLANNING—TO SET DIRECTION

a. 33 Strategies of War
b. Budget
c. 1990 Clean Air Act
d. 28-hour day

11. _____ can be regarded as an outcome of mental processes (cognitive process) leading to the selection of a course of action among several alternatives. Every _____ process produces a final choice. The output can be an action or an opinion of choice.

a. 33 Strategies of War
b. Decision making
c. 1990 Clean Air Act
d. 28-hour day

12. _____ is a term that refers both to:

- a formal discipline used to help appraise, or assess, the case for a project or proposal, which itself is a process known as project appraisal; and
- an informal approach to making decisions of any kind.

Under both definitions the process involves, whether explicitly or implicitly, weighing the total expected costs against the total expected benefits of one or more actions in order to choose the best or most profitable option. The formal process is often referred to as either CBA (_____) or BCost-benefit analysis

A hallmark of CBA is that all benefits and all costs are expressed in money terms, and are adjusted for the time value of money, so that all flows of benefits and flows of project costs over time (which tend to occur at different points in time) are expressed on a common basis in terms of their 'present value.' Closely related, but slightly different, formal techniques include Cost-effectiveness analysis, Economic impact analysis, Fiscal impact analysis and Social Return on Investment(SROI) analysis. The latter builds upon the logic of _____, but differs in that it is explicitly designed to inform the practical decision-making of enterprise managers and investors focused on optimising their social and environmental impacts.

a. Decision engineering
b. Gittins index
c. Kepner-Tregoe
d. Cost-benefit analysis

13. Appraisal is the third and last stage in using formal decision methods. The objective of the appraisal stage is for the decision maker to develop insight into the decision and determine a clear course of action. Much of the insight developed in this stage results from exploring the implications of the formal _____ developed during the formulation stage (i.e., from mining the model.)

Chapter 5. PLANNING—TO SET DIRECTION

a. Decision Matrix
b. Nominal group technique
c. Kepner-Tregoe
d. Decision model

14. _____ of the learning curve effect and the closely related experience curve effect express the relationship between equations for experience and efficiency or between efficiency gains and investment in the effort. The experience of 'learning curves' was first observed by the 19th Century German psychologist Hermann Ebbinghaus according to the difficulty of memorizing varying numbers of verbal stimuli, and subsequent learning about the complex processes of learning are discussed in the

.

The rule used for representing the learning curve effect states that the more times a task has been performed, the less time will be required on each subsequent iteration.

a. Distribution
b. Spatial Decision Support Systems
c. Point biserial correlation coefficient
d. Models

15. _____ has been described as the 'process of social influence in which one person can enlist the aid and support of others in the accomplishment of a common task' . A definition more inclusive of followers comes from Alan Keith of Genentech who said '_____ is ultimately about creating a way for people to contribute to making something extraordinary happen.'

_____ is one of the most salient aspects of the organizational context. However, defining _____ has been challenging.

a. Situational leadership
b. 1990 Clean Air Act
c. 28-hour day
d. Leadership

16. In decision theory and estimation theory, the _____ of an estimator, $\hat{\theta}$, of an unknown parameter of the distribution, θ, is the expected value of the loss function

$$R(\theta, \hat{\theta}) = \mathbb{E}_\theta L(\theta, \hat{\theta}) = \int L(\theta, \hat{\theta})\, dP_\theta.$$

where dP_θ is a probability measure parametrized by θ.

- For a scalar parameter θ and a quadratic loss function,

$$L(\theta, \hat{\theta}) = (\theta - \hat{\theta})^2$$

the _____ function becomes the mean squared error of the estimate,

$$R(\theta, \hat{\theta}) = E_\theta (\theta - \hat{\theta})^2$$

- In density estimation, the unknown parameter is probability density itself. The loss function is typically chosen to be a norm in an appropriate function space. For example, for L^2 norm,

$$L(f, \hat{f}) = \|f - \hat{f}\|_2^2$$

the _____ function becomes the mean integrated squared error

$$R(f, \hat{f}) = E\|f - \hat{f}\|^2$$

a. Linear model
b. Risk
c. Financial modeling
d. Risk aversion

17. _____ is a broad label that refers to any individuals or households that use goods and services generated within the economy. The concept of a _____ is used in different contexts, so that the usage and significance of the term may vary.

Typically when business people and economists talk of _____s they are talking about person as _____, an aggregated commodity item with little individuality other than that expressed in the buy/not-buy decision.

a. 1990 Clean Air Act
b. 28-hour day
c. 33 Strategies of War
d. Consumer

18. The _____ was enacted in 1972 by the United States Congress. It established the United States Consumer Product Safety Commission as an independent agency of the United States federal government and defined its basic authority. The act gives CPSC the power to develop safety standards and pursue recalls for products that present unreasonable or substantial risks of injury or death to consumers.
   a. 28-hour day
   b. 33 Strategies of War
   c. 1990 Clean Air Act
   d. Consumer Product Safety Act

19. _____ is the process of estimation in unknown situations. Prediction is a similar, but more general term. Both can refer to estimation of time series, cross-sectional or longitudinal data.
   a. 28-hour day
   b. 1990 Clean Air Act
   c. 33 Strategies of War
   d. Forecasting

20. _____ is a strategic planning method that some organizations use to make flexible long-term plans. It is in large part an adaptation and generalization of classic methods used by military intelligence.

The original method was that a group of analysts would generate simulation games for policy makers. In business applications, the emphasis on gaming the behavior of opponents was reduced (shifting more toward a game against nature). At Royal Dutch/Shell for example, _____ was viewed as changing mindsets about the exogenous part of the world, prior to formulating specific strategies.

   a. Retroactive overtime
   b. Labour productivity
   c. Time and attendance
   d. Scenario planning

21. The _____ is a chart that had been created by Bruce Henderson for the Boston Consulting Group in 1970 to help corporations with analyzing their business units or product lines. This helps the company allocate resources and is used as an analytical tool in brand marketing, product management, strategic management, and portfolio analysis. _____

Chapter 5. PLANNING—TO SET DIRECTION

To use the chart, analysts plot a scatter graph to rank the business units (or products) on the basis of their relative market shares and growth rates.

a. Market segment
b. Marketing plan
c. BCG matrix
d. Marketing strategy

22. _____ is the process of comparing the cost, cycle time, productivity, or quality of a specific process or method to another that is widely considered to be an industry standard or best practice. Essentially, _____ provides a snapshot of the performance of your business and helps you understand where you are in relation to a particular standard. The result is often a business case for making changes in order to make improvements.

a. Complementors
b. Cost leadership
c. Benchmarking
d. Competitive heterogeneity

Chapter 6. STRATEGIC MANAGEMENT AND ENTREPRENEURSHIP

1. _____ is, in very basic words, a position a firm occupies against its competitors.

According to Michael Porter, the three methods for creating a sustainable _____ are through:

1. Cost leadership

2. Differentiation

3. Focus (economics)

   a. Competitive advantage
   b. Theory Z
   c. 1990 Clean Air Act
   d. 28-hour day

2. _____ was a writer, management consultant, and self-described 'social ecologist.' Widely considered to be 'the father of modern management,' his 39 books and countless scholarly and popular articles explored how humans are organized across all sectors of society--in business, government and the nonprofit world. His writings have predicted many of the major developments of the late twentieth century, including privatization and decentralization; the rise of Japan to economic world power; the decisive importance of marketing; and the emergence of the information society with its necessity of lifelong learning. In 1959, Drucker coined the term 'knowledge worker' and later in his life considered knowledge work productivity to be the next frontier of management.
   a. Debora L. Spar
   b. Peter Ferdinand Drucker
   c. Chrissie Hynde
   d. Jacques Al-Salawat Nasruddin Nasser

3. Organizational culture is not the same as _____. It is wider and deeper concepts, something that an organization 'is' rather than what it 'has' (according to Buchanan and Huczynski.)

_____ is the total sum of the values, customs, traditions and meanings that make a company unique.

   a. Work design
   b. Path-goal theory
   c. Job analysis
   d. Corporate culture

Chapter 6. STRATEGIC MANAGEMENT AND ENTREPRENEURSHIP

4. _____ is a strategic planning method used to evaluate the Strengths, Weaknesses, Opportunities, and Threats involved in a project or in a business venture. It involves specifying the objective of the business venture or project and identifying the internal and external factors that are favorable and unfavorable to achieving that objective. The technique is credited to Albert Humphrey, who led a convention at Stanford University in the 1960s and 1970s using data from Fortune 500 companies.

a. Market share
b. Marketing
c. Corporate image
d. SWOT analysis

5. _____ is something that a firm can do well and that meets the following three conditions:

Competencies are things that companys execute well across several business units or product sectors.

Firms usually have few competencies, but these are usually less liable to change rapidly.

1. It provides consumer benefits
2. It is not easy for competitors to imitate
3. It can be leveraged widely to many products and markets.

A _____ can take various forms, including technical/subject matter know-how, a reliable process and/or close relationships with customers and suppliers (Mascarenhas et al. 1998.)

a. Core competency
b. Dominant Design
c. Learning-by-doing
d. NAIRU

6. _____ refers to the overarching strategy of the diversified firm. Such a _____ answers the questions of 'in which businesses should we be in?' and 'how does being in these business create synergy and/or add to the competitive advantage of the corporation as a whole?'

Business strategy refers to the aggregated strategies of single business firm or a strategic business unit (SBU) in a diversified corporation. According to Michael Porter, a firm must formulate a business strategy that incorporates either cost leadership, differentiation or focus in order to achieve a sustainable competitive advantage and long-term success in its chosen arenas or industries.

Chapter 6. STRATEGIC MANAGEMENT AND ENTREPRENEURSHIP

   a. Strategic group
   b. Strategic drift
   c. Competitive heterogeneity
   d. Corporate strategy

7. _____ is a type of trade policy that allows traders to act and transact without interference from government. Thus, the policy permits trading partners mutual gains from trade, with goods and services produced according to the theory of comparative advantage.

Under a _____ policy, prices are a reflection of true supply and demand, and are the sole determinant of resource allocation.

   a. 33 Strategies of War
   b. 1990 Clean Air Act
   c. 28-hour day
   d. Free Trade

8. _____ is understood as a business unit within the overall corporate identity which is distinguishable from other business because it serves a defined external market where management can conduct strategic planning in relation to products and markets. When companies become really large, they are best thought of as being composed of a number of businesses (or _____ s.)

In the broader domain of strategic management, the phrase '_____' came into use in the 1960s, largely as a result of General Electric's many units.

   a. Strategic group
   b. Switching cost
   c. Strategic drift
   d. Strategic business unit

9. _____ describes commerce transactions between businesses, such as between a manufacturer and a wholesaler, or between a wholesaler and a retailer. Contrasting terms are business-to-consumer (B2C) and business-to-government (B2G.)

The volume of B2B transactions is much higher than the volume of B2C transactions.

Chapter 6. STRATEGIC MANAGEMENT AND ENTREPRENEURSHIP

a. Product bundling
b. Category management
c. Market environment
d. Business-to-business

10. Business-to-consumer describes activities of businesses serving end consumers with products and/or services.

An example of a _____ transaction would be a person buying a pair of shoes from a retailer. The transactions that led to the shoes being available for purchase, that is the purchase of the leather, laces, rubber, etc.

a. Market environment
b. B2C
c. Green marketing
d. PEST analysis

11. _____, commonly referred to as 'eBusiness' or 'e-Business', may be defined as the utilization of information and communication technologies (ICT) in support of all the activities of business. Commerce constitutes the exchange of products and services between businesses, groups and individuals and hence can be seen as one of the essential activities of any business. Hence, electronic commerce or eCommerce focuses on the use of ICT to enable the external activities and relationships of the business with individuals, groups and other businesses.

a. AAAI
b. A4e
c. A Stake in the Outcome
d. Electronic business

12. A _____ is a formal relationship between two or more parties to pursue a set of agreed upon goals or to meet a critical business need while remaining independent organizations.

Partners may provide the _____ with resources such as products, distribution channels, manufacturing capability, project funding, capital equipment, knowledge, expertise, or intellectual property. The alliance is a cooperation or collaboration which aims for a synergy where each partner hopes that the benefits from the alliance will be greater than those from individual efforts.

a. Process automation
b. Farmshoring
c. Golden parachute
d. Strategic alliance

Chapter 6. STRATEGIC MANAGEMENT AND ENTREPRENEURSHIP

13. The _____ is a chart that had been created by Bruce Henderson for the Boston Consulting Group in 1970 to help corporations with analyzing their business units or product lines. This helps the company allocate resources and is used as an analytical tool in brand marketing, product management, strategic management, and portfolio analysis. _____

To use the chart, analysts plot a scatter graph to rank the business units (or products) on the basis of their relative market shares and growth rates.

   a. Marketing plan
   b. BCG matrix
   c. Marketing strategy
   d. Market segment

14. Procter is a surname, and may also refer to:

   - Bryan Waller Procter (pseud. Barry Cornwall), English poet
   - Goodwin Procter, American law firm
   - _____, consumer products multinational

   a. Downstream
   b. Strict liability
   c. Procter ' Gamble
   d. Master and Servant Acts

15. In economics, business, retail, and accounting, a _____ is the value of money that has been used up to produce something, and hence is not available for use anymore. In economics, a _____ is an alternative that is given up as a result of a decision. In business, the _____ may be one of acquisition, in which case the amount of money expended to acquire it is counted as _____.
   a. Fixed costs
   b. Cost allocation
   c. Cost overrun
   d. Cost

16. _____ is a concept developed by Michael Porter, used in business strategy. It describes a way to establish the competitive advantage. _____, in basic words, means the lowest cost of operation in the industry.

Chapter 6. STRATEGIC MANAGEMENT AND ENTREPRENEURSHIP

a. Cost leadership
b. Strategic group
c. Strategic business unit
d. Switching cost

17. The 'business case for _____', theorizes that in a global marketplace, a company that employs a diverse workforce (both men and women, people of many generations, people from ethnically and racially diverse backgrounds etc.) is better able to understand the demographics of the marketplace it serves and is thus better equipped to thrive in that marketplace than a company that has a more limited range of employee demographics.

An additional corollary suggests that a company that supports the _____ of its workforce can also improve employee satisfaction, productivity and retention.

a. Diversity
b. Trademark
c. Virtual team
d. Kanban

18. _____ is a method of working by adding to a project using many small (often unplanned) changes instead of a few (extensively planned) large jumps. Wikipedia, for example, illustrates the concept by building an encyclopedia bit by bit, continually adding to it. In a similar vein, it is said that Virgil wrote the Aeneid in an incremental process, averaging one line per day.

a. AAAI
b. A Stake in the Outcome
c. A4e
d. Incrementalism

19. _____ has been described as the 'process of social influence in which one person can enlist the aid and support of others in the accomplishment of a common task' . A definition more inclusive of followers comes from Alan Keith of Genentech who said '_____ is ultimately about creating a way for people to contribute to making something extraordinary happen.'

_____ is one of the most salient aspects of the organizational context. However, defining _____ has been challenging.

Chapter 6. STRATEGIC MANAGEMENT AND ENTREPRENEURSHIP

   a. 28-hour day
   b. 1990 Clean Air Act
   c. Situational leadership
   d. Leadership

20. A _____ is the term given to a company that facilitates the learning of its members and continuously transforms itself. _____s develop as a result of the pressures facing modern organizations and enables them to remain competitive in the business environment. A _____ has five main features; systems thinking, personal mastery, mental models, shared vision and team learning.
   a. Hoshin Kanri
   b. Learning organization
   c. Quality function deployment
   d. 1990 Clean Air Act

21. _____ is the set of processes, customs, policies, laws, and institutions affecting the way a corporation (or company) is directed, administered or controlled. _____ also includes the relationships among the many stakeholders involved and the goals for which the corporation is governed. The principal stakeholders are the shareholders/members, management, and the board of directors.
   a. Guarantee
   b. No-FEAR Act
   c. Flextime
   d. Corporate governance

22. _____ is an idea in the field of Organizational studies and management which describes the psychology, attitudes, experiences, beliefs and Values (personal and cultural values) of an organization. It has been defined as 'the specific collection of values and norms that are shared by people and groups in an organization and that control the way they interact with each other and with stakeholders outside the organization.'

This definition continues to explain organizational values also known as 'beliefs and ideas about what kinds of goals members of an organization should pursue and ideas about the appropriate kinds or standards of behavior organizational members should use to achieve these goals. From organizational values develop organizational norms, guidelines or expectations that prescribe appropriate kinds of behavior by employees in particular situations and control the behavior of organizational members towards one another.'

_____ is not the same as corporate culture.

Chapter 6. STRATEGIC MANAGEMENT AND ENTREPRENEURSHIP

a. Union shop
b. Organizational effectiveness
c. Organizational development
d. Organizational culture

23. _____ is a concept in ethics with several meanings. It is often used synonymously with such concepts as responsibility, answerability, enforcement, blameworthiness, liability and other terms associated with the expectation of account-giving. As an aspect of governance, it has been central to discussions related to problems in both the public and private (corporation) worlds.
   a. A Stake in the Outcome
   b. Accountability
   c. A4e
   d. Usury

24. _____ is an advertisement in which a particular product specifically mentions a competitor by name for the express purpose of showing why the competitor is inferior to the product naming it.

This should not be confused with parody advertisements, where a fictional product is being advertised for the purpose of poking fun at the particular advertisement, nor should it be confused with the use of a coined brand name for the purpose of comparing the product without actually naming an actual competitor. ('Wikipedia tastes better and is less filling than the Encyclopedia Galactica.')

In the 1980s, during what has been referred to as the cola wars, soft-drink manufacturer Pepsi ran a series of advertisements where people, caught on hidden camera, in a blind taste test, chose Pepsi over rival Coca-Cola.

   a. 1990 Clean Air Act
   b. Comparative advertising
   c. 33 Strategies of War
   d. 28-hour day

25. _____ is a form of corporate self-regulation integrated into a business model. Ideally, _____ policy would function as a built-in, self-regulating mechanism whereby business would monitor and ensure their adherence to law, ethical standards, and international norms. Business would embrace responsibility for the impact of their activities on the environment, consumers, employees, communities, stakeholders and all other members of the public sphere.
   a. 28-hour day
   b. 1990 Clean Air Act
   c. 33 Strategies of War
   d. Corporate social responsibility

Chapter 6. STRATEGIC MANAGEMENT AND ENTREPRENEURSHIP

26. A mutual _____ or stockholder is an individual or company (including a corporation) that legally owns one or more shares of stock in a joint stock company. A company's _____s collectively own that company. Thus, the typical goal of such companies is to enhance _____ value.
    a. Stockholder
    b. 1990 Clean Air Act
    c. Free riding
    d. Shareholder

27. _____ according to Onuoha (2007) is the practice of starting new organizations or revitalizing mature organizations, particularly new businesses generally in response to identified opportunities. _____ is often a difficult undertaking, as a vast majority of new businesses fail. Entrepreneurial activities are substantially different depending on the type of organization that is being started.
    a. AAAI
    b. Entrepreneurship
    c. A Stake in the Outcome
    d. A4e

28. _____ is a form of communication that typically attempts to persuade potential customers to purchase or to consume more of a particular brand of product or service. 'While now central to the contemporary global economy and the reproduction of global production networks, it is only quite recently that _____ has been more than a marginal influence on patterns of sales and production. The formation of modern _____ was intimately bound up with the emergence of new forms of monopoly capitalism around the end of the 19th and beginning of the 20th century as one element in corporate strategies to create, organize and where possible control markets, especially for mass produced consumer goods.
    a. A Stake in the Outcome
    b. AAAI
    c. A4e
    d. Advertising

29. A _____ is a business that is privately owned and operated, with a small number of employees and relatively low volume of sales. The legal definition of 'small' often varies by country and industry, but is generally under 100 employees in the United States and under 50 employees in the European Union. In comparison, the definition of mid-sized business by the number of employees is generally under 500 in the U.S. and 250 for the European Union.
    a. Pre-determined overhead rate
    b. Golden Boot Compensation
    c. Critical Success Factor
    d. Small Business

30. The _____ is a United States government agency that provides support to small businesses.

Chapter 6. STRATEGIC MANAGEMENT AND ENTREPRENEURSHIP

The mission of the _____ is 'to maintain and strengthen the nation's economy by enabling the establishment and viability of small businesses and by assisting in the economic recovery of communities after disasters.'

The _____ makes loans directly to businesses and acts as a guarantor on bank loans. In some circumstances it also makes loans to victims of natural disasters, works to get government procurement contracts for small businesses, and assists businesses with management, technical and training issues.

a. 28-hour day
b. 33 Strategies of War
c. 1990 Clean Air Act
d. Small Business Administration

31. A _____ is a formal statement of a set of business goals, the reasons why they are believed attainable, and the plan for reaching those goals. It may also contain background information about the organization or team attempting to reach those goals.

The business goals may be defined for for-profit or for non-profit organizations.

a. Time management
b. Distributed management
c. Crisis management
d. Business plan

32. _____ is the practice of using entrepreneurial skills without taking on the risks or accountability associated with entrepreneurial activities. It is practiced by employees within an established organization using a business model. Employees, perhaps engaged in a special project within a larger firm are supposed to behave as entrepreneurs, even though they have the resources and capabilities of the larger firm to draw upon.
a. A4e
b. A Stake in the Outcome
c. Intrapreneurship
d. AAAI

Chapter 7. CONTROLLING—TO ENSURE RESULTS

1. _____ is a broad label that refers to any individuals or households that use goods and services generated within the economy. The concept of a _____ is used in different contexts, so that the usage and significance of the term may vary.

Typically when business people and economists talk of _____s they are talking about person as _____, an aggregated commodity item with little individuality other than that expressed in the buy/not-buy decision.

   a. 33 Strategies of War
   b. 28-hour day
   c. 1990 Clean Air Act
   d. Consumer

2. The _____ was enacted in 1972 by the United States Congress. It established the United States Consumer Product Safety Commission as an independent agency of the United States federal government and defined its basic authority. The act gives CPSC the power to develop safety standards and pursue recalls for products that present unreasonable or substantial risks of injury or death to consumers.
   a. 28-hour day
   b. 1990 Clean Air Act
   c. 33 Strategies of War
   d. Consumer Product Safety Act

3. _____ is one of the managerial functions like planning, organizing, staffing and directing. It is an important function because it helps to check the errors and to take the corrective action so that deviation from standards are minimized and stated goals of the organization are achieved in desired manner. According to modern concepts, _____ is a foreseeing action whereas earlier concept of _____ was used only when errors were detected. _____ in management means setting standards, measuring actual performance and taking corrective action.
   a. Turnover
   b. Control
   c. Schedule of reinforcement
   d. Decision tree pruning

4. A _____ is a change implemented to address a weakness identified in a management system. Normally _____s are implemented in response to a customer complaint, abnormal levels of internal nonconformity, nonconformities identified during an internal audit or adverse or unstable trends in product and process monitoring such as would be identified by SPC.

The process of determining a _____ requires identification of actions that can be taken to prevent or mitigate the weakness.

a. Zero defects
b. 1990 Clean Air Act
c. 28-hour day
d. Corrective action

5. _____ is the process whereby an organization establishes the parameters within which programs, investments, and acquisitions are reaching the desired results. Performance Reference Model of the Federal Enterprise Architecture, 2005.

This process of measuring performance often requires the use of statistical evidence to determine progress toward specific defined organizational objectives.

There are many types of measurements.

a. Workflow
b. Performance measurement
c. Crisis management
d. CIFMS

6. _____ refers to the movement of cash into or out of a business or financial product. It is usually measured during a specified, finite period of time. Measurement of _____ can be used

- to determine a project's rate of return or value. The time of _____s into and out of projects are used as inputs in financial models such as internal rate of return, and net present value.
- to determine problems with a business's liquidity. Being profitable does not necessarily mean being liquid. A company can fail because of a shortage of cash, even while profitable.
- as an alternate measure of a business's profits when it is believed that accrual accounting concepts do not represent economic realities. For example, a company may be notionally profitable but generating little operational cash (as may be the case for a company that barters its products rather than selling for cash.) In such a case, the company may be deriving additional operating cash by issuing shares evaluating default risk, re-investment requirements, etc.

_____ is a generic term used differently depending on the context. It may be defined by users for their own purposes.

a. Cash flow
b. Gross profit margin
c. Gross profit
d. Sweat equity

Chapter 7. CONTROLLING—TO ENSURE RESULTS

7. _____ has been described as the 'process of social influence in which one person can enlist the aid and support of others in the accomplishment of a common task' . A definition more inclusive of followers comes from Alan Keith of Genentech who said '_____ is ultimately about creating a way for people to contribute to making something extraordinary happen.'

_____ is one of the most salient aspects of the organizational context. However, defining _____ has been challenging.

   a. Leadership
   b. 1990 Clean Air Act
   c. 28-hour day
   d. Situational leadership

8. _____ is a 'policy by which management devotes its time to investigating only those situations in which actual results differ significantly from planned results. The idea is that management should spend its valuable time concentrating on the more important items (such as shaping the company's future strategic course.) Attention is given only to material deviations requiring investigation.'

It is not entirely synonymous with the concept of exception management in that it describes a policy where absolute focus is on exception management, in contrast to moderate application of exception management.

   a. Management by exception
   b. C-A-K-E
   c. Business philosophy
   d. Trustee

9. _____ describes the situation when output from (or information about the result of) an event or phenomenon in the past will influence the same event/phenomenon in the present or future. When an event is part of a chain of cause-and-effect that forms a circuit or loop, then the event is said to 'feed back' into itself.

_____ is also a synonym for:

   - _____ signal; the information about the initial event that is the basis for subsequent modification of the event.
   - _____ loop; the causal path that leads from the initial generation of the _____ signal to the subsequent modification of the event.

_____ is a mechanism, process or signal that is looped back to control a system within itself. Such a loop is called a _____ loop.

Chapter 7. CONTROLLING—TO ENSURE RESULTS

a. 1990 Clean Air Act
b. Feedback
c. Feedback loop
d. Positive feedback

10. In accounting and auditing, _____ is defined as a process effected by an organization's structure, work and authority flows, people and management information systems, designed to help the organization accomplish specific goals or objectives. It is a means by which an organization's resources are directed, monitored, and measured. It plays an important role in preventing and detecting fraud and protecting the organization's resources, both physical (e.g., machinery and property) and intangible (e.g., reputation or intellectual property such as trademarks.)

a. Audit committee
b. Internal control
c. A Stake in the Outcome
d. Internal auditing

11. _____ is a process of planning and controlling the performance or execution of any type of activity, such as:

- a project (project _____) or
- a process (process _____, sometimes referred to as the process performance measurement and management system.)

Organization's senior management is responsible for carrying out its _____.

a. Human Relations Movement
b. Participatory management
c. Work design
d. Management process

12. Procter is a surname, and may also refer to:

- Bryan Waller Procter (pseud. Barry Cornwall), English poet
- Goodwin Procter, American law firm
- _____, consumer products multinational

Chapter 7. CONTROLLING—TO ENSURE RESULTS

   a. Downstream
   b. Strict liability
   c. Master and Servant Acts
   d. Procter ' Gamble

13. _____ refers to an assessment of the viability, stability and profitability of a business, sub-business or project.

It is performed by professionals who prepare reports using ratios that make use of information taken from financial statements and other reports. These reports are usually presented to top management as one of their bases in making business decisions.

   a. 28-hour day
   b. 33 Strategies of War
   c. 1990 Clean Air Act
   d. Financial analysis

14. _____ is a system of discipline where the penalties increase upon repeat occurrences.

This term is often used in an employment or human resources context where rather than terminating employees for first or minor infractions, there is a system of escalating responses intended to correct the negative behaviour rather than to punish the employee.

The typical stages of _____ in a workplace are:

   1. Counselling or a verbal warning;
   2. A written warning;
   3. Suspension or demotion; and
   4. Termination.

The stage chosen for a particular infraction will depend on a variety of factors that include the severity of the infraction, the previous work history of the employee and how the choice will affect others in the organization.

   a. Performance appraisal
   b. Human resource management
   c. Salary
   d. Progressive discipline

Chapter 7. CONTROLLING—TO ENSURE RESULTS

15. _____ is an area of business concerned with the production of goods and services, and involves the responsibility of ensuring that business operations are efficient in terms of using as little resource as needed, and effective in terms of meeting customer requirements. It is concerned with managing the process that converts inputs (in the forms of materials, labour and energy) into outputs (in the form of goods and services.)

Operations traditionally refers to the production of goods and services separately, although the distinction between these two main types of operations is increasingly difficult to make as manufacturers tend to merge product and service offerings.

 a. AAAI
 b. A Stake in the Outcome
 c. A4e
 d. Operations management

16. _____ is the level of inventory that minimizes the total inventory holding costs and ordering costs. The framework used to determine this order quantity is also known as Wilson _____ Model. The model was developed by F. W. Harris in 1913.
 a. Anti-leadership
 b. Event management
 c. Effective executive
 d. Economic order quantity

17. _____ is an inventory strategy that strives to improve the return on investment of a business by reducing in-process inventory and its associated carrying costs. To meet _____ objectives, the process relies on signals between different points in the process. This means the process is often driven by a series of signals, or Kanban , which tell production when to make the next part. Kanban are usually 'tickets' but can be simple visual signals, such as the presence or absence of a part on a shelf. Implemented correctly, _____ can dramatically improve a manufacturing organization's return on investment, quality, and efficiency.
 a. 33 Strategies of War
 b. 1990 Clean Air Act
 c. Just-in-time
 d. 28-hour day

18. _____ is a concept related to lean and just-in-time (JIT) production. The Japanese word _____ is a common term meaning 'signboard' or 'billboard'. According to Taiichi Ohno, the man credited with developing JIT, _____ is a means through which JIT is achieved.

Chapter 7. CONTROLLING—TO ENSURE RESULTS

   a. Trademark
   b. Risk management
   c. Kanban
   d. Succession planning

19. In engineering and manufacturing, _____ and quality engineering are used in developing systems to ensure products or services are designed and produced to meet or exceed customer requirements. Refer to the definition by Merriam-Webster for further information . These systems are often developed in conjunction with other business and engineering disciplines using a cross-functional approach.

   a. Single Minute Exchange of Die
   b. Statistical process control
   c. Process capability
   d. Quality control

20. _____ is a business management strategy, initially implemented by Motorola, that today enjoys widespread application in many sectors of industry.

_____ seeks to improve the quality of process outputs by identifying and removing the causes of defects (errors) and variation in manufacturing and business processes. It uses a set of quality management methods, including statistical methods, and creates a special infrastructure of people within the organization ('Black Belts' etc.)

   a. Theory of constraints
   b. Production line
   c. Takt time
   d. Six Sigma

21. _____ is a process of agreeing upon objectives within an organization so that management and employees agree to the objectives and understand what they are in the organization.

The term '_____' was first popularized by Peter Drucker in his 1954 book 'The Practice of Management'.

The essence of _____ is participative goal setting, choosing course of actions and decision making.

   a. Clean sheet review
   b. Business economics
   c. Job enrichment
   d. Management by objectives

22. The U.S. _____ is an independent agency of the United States government which holds primary responsibility for enforcing the federal securities laws and regulating the securities industry, the nation's stock and options exchanges, and other electronic securities markets. The SEC was created by section 4 of the Securities Exchange Act of 1934 (now codified as 15 U.S.C. Â§ 78d and commonly referred to as the 1934 Act.)
   a. 33 Strategies of War
   b. 28-hour day
   c. 1990 Clean Air Act
   d. Securities and Exchange Commission

Chapter 8. ORGANIZING—TO CREATE STRUCTURES

1. _____ was a writer, management consultant, and self-described 'social ecologist.' Widely considered to be 'the father of modern management,' his 39 books and countless scholarly and popular articles explored how humans are organized across all sectors of society--in business, government and the nonprofit world. His writings have predicted many of the major developments of the late twentieth century, including privatization and decentralization; the rise of Japan to economic world power; the decisive importance of marketing; and the emergence of the information society with its necessity of lifelong learning. In 1959, Drucker coined the term 'knowledge worker' and later in his life considered knowledge work productivity to be the next frontier of management.
   a. Chrissie Hynde
   b. Debora L. Spar
   c. Jacques Al-Salawat Nasruddin Nasser
   d. Peter Ferdinand Drucker

2. The _____ is the labour pool in employment. It is generally used to describe those working for a single company or industry, but can also apply to a geographic region like a city, country, state, etc. The term generally excludes the employers or management, and implies those involved in manual labour.
   a. Division of labour
   b. Work-life balance
   c. Pink-collar worker
   d. Workforce

3. _____ is a type of trade policy that allows traders to act and transact without interference from government. Thus, the policy permits trading partners mutual gains from trade, with goods and services produced according to the theory of comparative advantage.

Under a _____ policy, prices are a reflection of true supply and demand, and are the sole determinant of resource allocation.

   a. 28-hour day
   b. 1990 Clean Air Act
   c. 33 Strategies of War
   d. Free Trade

Chapter 8. ORGANIZING—TO CREATE STRUCTURES

4. _____ is an increasingly broadening term with which an organization, or other human system describes the combination of traditionally administrative personnel functions with acquisition and application of skills, knowledge and experience, Employee Relations and resource planning at various levels. The field draws upon concepts developed in Industrial/Organizational Psychology and System Theory. _____ has at least two related interpretations depending on context. The original usage derives from political economy and economics, where it was traditionally called labor, one of four factors of production although this perspective is changing as a function of new and ongoing research into more strategic approaches at national levels. This first usage is used more in terms of '_____ development', and can go beyond just organizations to the level of nations . The more traditional usage within corporations and businesses refers to the individuals within a firm or agency, and to the portion of the organization that deals with hiring, firing, training, and other personnel issues, typically referred to as `_____ management'.

   a. Human resource management
   b. Human resources
   c. Progressive discipline
   d. Bradford Factor

5. _____, widely known as F. W. Taylor, was an American mechanical engineer who sought to improve industrial efficiency. He is regarded as the father of scientific management, and was one of the first management consultants.

Taylor was one of the intellectual leaders of the Efficiency Movement and his ideas, broadly conceived, were highly influential in the Progressive Era.

   a. Douglas N. Daft
   b. Jonah Jacob Goldberg
   c. Geoffrey Colvin
   d. Frederick Winslow Taylor

6. A _____ is a group of employees from various functional areas of the organization - research, engineering, marketing, finance. human resources, and operations, for example - who are all focused on a specific objective and are responsible to work as a team to improve coordination and innovation across divisions and resolve mutual problems.

   a. Sociotechnical systems
   b. Graduate recruitment
   c. Goal-setting theory
   d. Cross-functional team

7. _____ is a term that was popularized by renowned psychologist David McClelland in 1961. However, it should be recognized that McClellend's thinking was strongly influenced by the pioneering work of Henry Murray who first identified underlying psychological human needs and motivational processes (1938.) It was Murray who set out a taxonomy of needs, including Achievement, Power and Affiliation - and placed these in the context of an integrated motivational model.

Chapter 8. ORGANIZING—TO CREATE STRUCTURES

   a. Two-factor theory
   b. 1990 Clean Air Act
   c. Need for Achievement
   d. Need for Power

8. A _____ is a contemporary apporach to organizational design. It is an organization that is not defined by, or limited to, the horizontal, vertical, or external boundaries imposed by a predefined structure. This term was coined by former GE chairman Jack Welch because he wanted to eliminate vertical and horizontal boundaries within GE and break down external barriers between the company and its customers and suppliers.

   a. Headquarters
   b. Business Roundtable
   c. Chief risk officer
   d. Boundaryless organization

9. _____ comprises a range of practices used in an organisation to identify, create, represent, distribute and enable adoption of insights and experiences. Such insights and experiences comprise knowledge, either embodied in individuals or embedded in organisational processes or practice.

An established discipline since 1991 , _____ includes courses taught in the fields of business administration, information systems, management, and library and information sciences .

   a. 28-hour day
   b. 1990 Clean Air Act
   c. 33 Strategies of War
   d. Knowledge management

10. _____ is an advertisement in which a particular product specifically mentions a competitor by name for the express purpose of showing why the competitor is inferior to the product naming it.

This should not be confused with parody advertisements, where a fictional product is being advertised for the purpose of poking fun at the particular advertisement, nor should it be confused with the use of a coined brand name for the purpose of comparing the product without actually naming an actual competitor. ('Wikipedia tastes better and is less filling than the Encyclopedia Galactica.')

In the 1980s, during what has been referred to as the cola wars, soft-drink manufacturer Pepsi ran a series of advertisements where people, caught on hidden camera, in a blind taste test, chose Pepsi over rival Coca-Cola.

a. Comparative advertising
b. 33 Strategies of War
c. 1990 Clean Air Act
d. 28-hour day

11. The term '_____' refers to the concept of collecting information and attempting to spot a pattern in the information. In some fields of study, the term '_____' has more formally-defined meanings.

In project management _____ is a mathematical technique that uses historical results to predict future outcome.

a. Trend analysis
b. Regression analysis
c. Least squares
d. Stepwise regression

12. _____ is one of the managerial functions like planning, organizing, staffing and directing. It is an important function because it helps to check the errors and to take the corrective action so that deviation from standards are minimized and stated goals of the organization are achieved in desired manner. According to modern concepts, _____ is a foreseeing action whereas earlier concept of _____ was used only when errors were detected. _____ in management means setting standards, measuring actual performance and taking corrective action.

a. Control
b. Turnover
c. Schedule of reinforcement
d. Decision tree pruning

13. _____ has been described as the 'process of social influence in which one person can enlist the aid and support of others in the accomplishment of a common task'. A definition more inclusive of followers comes from Alan Keith of Genentech who said '_____ is ultimately about creating a way for people to contribute to making something extraordinary happen.'

_____ is one of the most salient aspects of the organizational context. However, defining _____ has been challenging.

a. Situational leadership
b. Leadership
c. 28-hour day
d. 1990 Clean Air Act

Chapter 8. ORGANIZING—TO CREATE STRUCTURES

14. _____ is a term originating in military organization theory, but now used more commonly in business management, particularly human resource management. _____ refers to the number of subordinates a supervisor has.

In the hierarchical business organization of the past it was not uncommon to see average spans of 1 to 10 or even less. That is, one manager supervised ten employees on average.

   a. Mentoring
   b. CIFMS
   c. Senior management
   d. Span of control

15. _____ is the process by which the activities of an organisation, particularly those regarding decision-making, become concentrated within a particular location and/or group.
   a. Corner office
   b. Product innovation
   c. Chief operating officer
   d. Centralization

16. _____ is the process of dispersing decision-making governance closer to the people or citizen. It includes the dispersal of administration or governance in sectors or areas like engineering, management science, political science, political economy, sociology and economics. _____ is also possible in the dispersal of population and employment.
   a. Frenemy
   b. Business plan
   c. Formula for Change
   d. Decentralization

Chapter 9. ORGANIZATIONAL CULTURE AND DESIGN

1. _____ is an idea in the field of Organizational studies and management which describes the psychology, attitudes, experiences, beliefs and Values (personal and cultural values) of an organization. It has been defined as 'the specific collection of values and norms that are shared by people and groups in an organization and that control the way they interact with each other and with stakeholders outside the organization.'

This definition continues to explain organizational values also known as 'beliefs and ideas about what kinds of goals members of an organization should pursue and ideas about the appropriate kinds or standards of behavior organizational members should use to achieve these goals. From organizational values develop organizational norms, guidelines or expectations that prescribe appropriate kinds of behavior by employees in particular situations and control the behavior of organizational members towards one another.'

_____ is not the same as corporate culture.

   a. Organizational development
   b. Organizational culture
   c. Organizational effectiveness
   d. Union shop

2. _____ is a process of agreeing upon objectives within an organization so that management and employees agree to the objectives and understand what they are in the organization.

The term '_____' was first popularized by Peter Drucker in his 1954 book 'The Practice of Management'.

The essence of _____ is participative goal setting, choosing course of actions and decision making.

   a. Clean sheet review
   b. Business economics
   c. Job enrichment
   d. Management by objectives

3. _____ is a strategic planning method used to evaluate the Strengths, Weaknesses, Opportunities, and Threats involved in a project or in a business venture. It involves specifying the objective of the business venture or project and identifying the internal and external factors that are favorable and unfavorable to achieving that objective. The technique is credited to Albert Humphrey, who led a convention at Stanford University in the 1960s and 1970s using data from Fortune 500 companies.
   a. Corporate image
   b. Market share
   c. Marketing
   d. SWOT analysis

Chapter 9. ORGANIZATIONAL CULTURE AND DESIGN

4. _____ is an advertisement in which a particular product specifically mentions a competitor by name for the express purpose of showing why the competitor is inferior to the product naming it.

This should not be confused with parody advertisements, where a fictional product is being advertised for the purpose of poking fun at the particular advertisement, nor should it be confused with the use of a coined brand name for the purpose of comparing the product without actually naming an actual competitor. ('Wikipedia tastes better and is less filling than the Encyclopedia Galactica.')

In the 1980s, during what has been referred to as the cola wars, soft-drink manufacturer Pepsi ran a series of advertisements where people, caught on hidden camera, in a blind taste test, chose Pepsi over rival Coca-Cola.

   a. 28-hour day
   b. 1990 Clean Air Act
   c. 33 Strategies of War
   d. Comparative advertising

5. The 'business case for _____', theorizes that in a global marketplace, a company that employs a diverse workforce (both men and women, people of many generations, people from ethnically and racially diverse backgrounds etc.) is better able to understand the demographics of the marketplace it serves and is thus better equipped to thrive in that marketplace than a company that has a more limited range of employee demographics.

An additional corollary suggests that a company that supports the _____ of its workforce can also improve employee satisfaction, productivity and retention.

   a. Virtual team
   b. Diversity
   c. Trademark
   d. Kanban

6. _____ has been described as the 'process of social influence in which one person can enlist the aid and support of others in the accomplishment of a common task' . A definition more inclusive of followers comes from Alan Keith of Genentech who said '_____ is ultimately about creating a way for people to contribute to making something extraordinary happen.'

_____ is one of the most salient aspects of the organizational context. However, defining _____ has been challenging.

Chapter 9. ORGANIZATIONAL CULTURE AND DESIGN

a. 28-hour day
b. Situational leadership
c. 1990 Clean Air Act
d. Leadership

7. _____ consists of the processes a company uses to track and organize its contacts with its current and prospective customers. _____ software is used to support these processes; information about customers and customer interactions can be entered, stored and accessed by employees in different company departments. Typical _____ goals are to improve services provided to customers, and to use customer contact information for targeted marketing.
   a. Disruptive technology
   b. Green marketing
   c. Customer relationship management
   d. Marketing plan

8. A _____ is the system of organizations, people, technology, activities, information and resources involved in moving a product or service from supplier to customer. _____ activities transform natural resources, raw materials and components into a finished product that is delivered to the end customer. In sophisticated _____ systems, used products may re-enter the _____ at any point where residual value is recyclable.
   a. Wholesalers
   b. Drop shipping
   c. Packaging
   d. Supply chain

9. _____ is the management of a network of interconnected businesses involved in the ultimate provision of product and service packages required by end customers (Harland, 1996.) _____ spans all movement and storage of raw materials, work-in-process inventory, and finished goods from point of origin to point of consumption (supply chain.)

The definition an American professional association put forward is that _____ encompasses the planning and management of all activities involved in sourcing, procurement, conversion, and logistics management activities.

   a. Drop shipping
   b. Freight forwarder
   c. Packaging
   d. Supply chain management

Chapter 9. ORGANIZATIONAL CULTURE AND DESIGN

10. In management science, operations research and organizational development (OD), human organizations are viewed as systems (conceptual systems) of interacting components such as _____ or system aggregates, which are carriers of numerous complex processes and organizational structures. Organizational development theorist Peter Senge developed the notion of organizations as systems in his book The Fifth Discipline.

Systems thinking is a style of thinking/reasoning and problem solving.

   a. 28-hour day
   b. Systems thinking
   c. 1990 Clean Air Act
   d. Subsystems

11. The _____ is a monograph published by Frederick Winslow Taylor in 1911. This influential monograph is the basis of modern organization and decision theory and has motivated administrators and students of managerial technique. Taylor was an American mechanical engineer and a management consultant in his later years.
   a. 28-hour day
   b. 1990 Clean Air Act
   c. Principles of Scientific Management
   d. 33 Strategies of War

12. _____ is a theory of management that analyzes and synthesizes workflows, with the objective of improving labour productivity. The core ideas of the theory were developed by Frederick Winslow Taylor in the 1880s and 1890s, and were first published in his monographs, Shop Management and The Principles of _____ Taylor believed that decisions based upon tradition and rules of thumb should be replaced by precise procedures developed after careful study of an individual at work.
   a. Master production schedule
   b. Value engineering
   c. Capacity planning
   d. Scientific Management

13.

_____ is a systematic method to improve the 'value' of goods or products and services by using an examination of function. Value, as defined, is the ratio of function to cost. Value can therefore be increased by either improving the function or reducing the cost.

a. Cellular manufacturing
b. Value engineering
c. Capacity planning
d. Master production schedule

Chapter 10. HUMAN RESOURCE SYSTEMS

1. The 'business case for _____', theorizes that in a global marketplace, a company that employs a diverse workforce (both men and women, people of many generations, people from ethnically and racially diverse backgrounds etc.) is better able to understand the demographics of the marketplace it serves and is thus better equipped to thrive in that marketplace than a company that has a more limited range of employee demographics.

An additional corollary suggests that a company that supports the _____ of its workforce can also improve employee satisfaction, productivity and retention.

   a. Trademark
   b. Kanban
   c. Virtual team
   d. Diversity

2. _____ is an increasingly broadening term with which an organization, or other human system describes the combination of traditionally administrative personnel functions with acquisition and application of skills, knowledge and experience, Employee Relations and resource planning at various levels. The field draws upon concepts developed in Industrial/Organizational Psychology and System Theory. _____ has at least two related interpretations depending on context. The original usage derives from political economy and economics, where it was traditionally called labor, one of four factors of production although this perspective is changing as a function of new and ongoing research into more strategic approaches at national levels. This first usage is used more in terms of '_____ development', and can go beyond just organizations to the level of nations. The more traditional usage within corporations and businesses refers to the individuals within a firm or agency, and to the portion of the organization that deals with hiring, firing, training, and other personnel issues, typically referred to as `_____ management'.
   a. Progressive discipline
   b. Bradford Factor
   c. Human resources
   d. Human resource management

3. _____ is a contract between two parties, one being the employer and the other being the employee. An employee may be defined as: 'A person in the service of another under any contract of hire, express or implied, oral or written, where the employer has the power or right to control and direct the employee in the material details of how the work is to be performed.' Black's Law Dictionary page 471 (5th ed. 1979.)
   a. Exit interview
   b. Employment counsellor
   c. Employment rate
   d. Employment

4. The term _____ was created by President Lyndon B. Johnson when he signed Executive Order 11246 on September 24, 1965, created to prohibit federal contractors from discriminating against employees on the basis of race, sex, creed, religion, color, or national origin. In more recent times, most employers have also added sexual orientation to the list of non-discrimination.

Chapter 10. HUMAN RESOURCE SYSTEMS

The Executive Order also required contractors to implement affirmative action plans to increase the participation of minorities and women in the workplace.

   a. AAAI
   b. A Stake in the Outcome
   c. A4e
   d. Equal Employment Opportunity

5. _____ is a cross-disciplinary area concerned with protecting the safety, health and welfare of people engaged in work or employment. The goal of all _____ programs is to foster a work free safe environment. As a secondary effect, it may also protect co-workers, family members, employers, customers, suppliers, nearby communities, and other members of the public who are impacted by the workplace environment.
   a. AAAI
   b. A4e
   c. A Stake in the Outcome
   d. Occupational Safety and Health

6. The _____ is the primary federal law which governs occupational health and safety in the private sector and federal government in the United States. It was enacted by Congress in 1970 and was signed by President Richard Nixon on December 29, 1970. Its main goal is to ensure that employers provide employees with an environment free from recognized hazards, such as exposure to toxic chemicals, excessive noise levels, mechanical dangers, heat or cold stress, or unsanitary conditions.
   a. Unemployment Action Center
   b. Unemployment and Farm Relief Act
   c. Occupational Safety and Health Act
   d. United States Department of Justice

7.

The terms _____ and positive action refer to policies that take race, ethnicity, or gender into consideration in an attempt to promote equal opportunity. The focus of such policies ranges from employment and education to public contracting and health programs. The impetus towards _____ is twofold: to maximize diversity in all levels of society, along with its presumed benefits, and to redress perceived disadvantages due to overt, institutional, or involuntary discrimination.

Chapter 10. HUMAN RESOURCE SYSTEMS

   a. Adam Smith
   b. Affiliation
   c. Abraham Harold Maslow
   d. Affirmative action

8. The _____ of 1967, Pub. L. No. 90-202, 81 Stat. 602 (Dec. 15, 1967), codified as Chapter 14 of Title 29 of the United States Code, 29 U.S.C. § 621 through 29 U.S.C. § 634 (ADEA), prohibits employment discrimination against persons 40 years of age or older in the United States). The law also sets standards for pensions and benefits provided by employers and requires that information about the needs of older workers be provided to the general public.
   a. Undue hardship
   b. Extra time
   c. Unemployment and Farm Relief Act
   d. Age Discrimination in Employment Act

9. The _____ of 1990 (ADA) is the short title of United States (Pub.L. 101-336, 104 Stat. 327, enacted July 26, 1990), codified at 42 U.S.C. § 12101 et seq. It was signed into law on July 26, 1990, by President George H. W. Bush, and later amended with changes effective January 1, 2009. The ADA is a wide-ranging civil rights law that prohibits, under certain circumstances, discrimination based on disability. It affords similar protections against discrimination to Americans with disabilities as the Civil Rights Act of 1964,
   a. Employment discrimination
   b. Equal Pay Act of 1963
   c. Australian labour law
   d. Americans with Disabilities Act

10. The _____ is a United States labor law allowing an employee to take unpaid leave due to a serious health condition that makes the employee unable to perform his job or to care for a sick family member or to care for a new son or daughter (including by birth, adoption or foster care.) The bill was among the first signed into law by President Bill Clinton in his first term.
   a. Harvester Judgment
   b. Family and Medical Leave Act of 1993
   c. Contributory negligence
   d. Sarbanes-Oxley Act of 2002

Chapter 10. HUMAN RESOURCE SYSTEMS

11. _____ occurs when expectant women are fired, not hired, or otherwise discriminated against due to their pregnancy or intention to become pregnant. Common forms of _____ include not being hired due to visible pregnancy or likelihood of becoming pregnant, being fired after informing an employer of one's pregnancy, being fired after maternity leave, and receiving a pay dock due to pregnancy. In the United States, since 1978, employers are legally bound to provide what insurance, leave pay, and additional support that would be bestowed upon any employee with medical leave or disability.

   a. 28-hour day
   b. 1990 Clean Air Act
   c. 33 Strategies of War
   d. Pregnancy Discrimination

12. _____ is an advertisement in which a particular product specifically mentions a competitor by name for the express purpose of showing why the competitor is inferior to the product naming it.

This should not be confused with parody advertisements, where a fictional product is being advertised for the purpose of poking fun at the particular advertisement, nor should it be confused with the use of a coined brand name for the purpose of comparing the product without actually naming an actual competitor. ('Wikipedia tastes better and is less filling than the Encyclopedia Galactica.')

In the 1980s, during what has been referred to as the cola wars, soft-drink manufacturer Pepsi ran a series of advertisements where people, caught on hidden camera, in a blind taste test, chose Pepsi over rival Coca-Cola.

   a. 33 Strategies of War
   b. 28-hour day
   c. 1990 Clean Air Act
   d. Comparative advertising

13. In employment law, a (BFOQ) (US) or bona fide occupational requirement (BFOR) (Canada) is a quality or an attribute that employers are allowed to consider when making decisions on the hiring and retention of employees - qualities that, when considered, in other contexts would be considered discriminatory and thus violating civil rights employment law.

In employment discrimination law in the United States, United States Code Title 29 , Chapter 14 (age discrimination in employment), section 623 (prohibition of age discrimination) establishes that 'It shall not be unlawful for an employer, employment agency, or labor organization (1) to take any action otherwise prohibited under subsections (a), (b), (c), or (e) of this section where age is a _____ reasonably necessary to the normal operation of the particular business, or where the differentiation is based on reasonable factors other than age, or where such practices involve an employee in a workplace in a foreign country, and compliance with such subsections would cause such employer, or a corporation controlled by such employer, to violate the laws of the country in which such workplace is located.'

One example of _____s are mandatory retirement ages for bus drivers and airline pilots, for safety reasons. Further, in advertising, a manufacturer of men's clothing may lawfully advertise for male models.

   a. Sick leave
   b. MacPherson v. Buick Motor Co.
   c. Corporate governance
   d. Bona fide occupational qualification

14. _____ is unwelcome harassment of a sexual nature, or based upon the receiving party's sex or gender. In some contexts or circumstances, _____ may be illegal. It includes a range of behavior from seemingly mild transgressions and annoyances to actual sexual abuse or sexual assault.
   a. 28-hour day
   b. 1990 Clean Air Act
   c. Hypernorms
   d. Sexual harassment

15. The _____ 1970 is an Act of the United Kingdom Parliament which prohibits any less favourable treatment between men and women in terms of pay and conditions of employment. It came into force on 29 December 1975. The term pay is interpreted in a broad sense to include, on top of wages, things like holidays, pension rights, company perks and some kinds of bonuses.
   a. Equal Pay Act
   b. Architectural Barriers Act of 1968
   c. Oncale v. Sundowner Offshore Services
   d. Australian labour law

16. The _____, Pub. L. No. 88-38, 77 Stat. 56, (June 10, 1963) codified at 29 U.S.C. § 206(d), is a United States federal law amending the Fair Labor Standards Act, aimed at abolishing wage differentials based on sex. In passing the bill, Congress denounces sex discrimination.
   a. Invitee
   b. Architectural Barriers Act of 1968
   c. Extra time
   d. Equal Pay Act of 1963

17. An _____ is a natural person, business, or corporation which provides goods or services to another entity under terms specified in a contract or within a verbal agreement. Unlike an employee, an _____ does not work regularly for an employer but works as and when required, during which time she or he may be subject to the Law of Agency. _____s are usually paid on a freelance basis.

a. Equal Pay Act of 1963
b. Independent contractor
c. Occupational Safety and Health Act
d. Employment protection legislation

18. _____ refers to the process of screening, and selecting qualified people for a job at an organization or firm mid- and large-size organizations and companies often retain professional recruiters or outsource some of the process to _____ agencies. External _____ is the process of attracting and selecting employees from outside the organization.

The _____ industry has four main types of agencies: employment agencies, _____ websites and job search engines, 'headhunters' for executive and professional _____, and in-house _____.

a. Referral recruitment
b. Recruitment Process Outsourcing
c. Labour hire
d. Recruitment

19. A _____ is a process in which a potential employee is evaluated by an employer for prospective employment in their company, organization and was established in the late 16th century.

A _____ typically precedes the hiring decision, and is used to evaluate the candidate. The interview is usually preceded by the evaluation of submitted résumés from interested candidates, then selecting a small number of candidates for interviews.

a. Split shift
b. Payrolling
c. Supported employment
d. Job interview

20. The U.S. _____ is an independent agency of the United States government which holds primary responsibility for enforcing the federal securities laws and regulating the securities industry, the nation's stock and options exchanges, and other electronic securities markets. The SEC was created by section 4 of the Securities Exchange Act of 1934 (now codified as 15 U.S.C. Â§ 78d and commonly referred to as the 1934 Act.)

a. Securities and Exchange Commission
b. 33 Strategies of War
c. 1990 Clean Air Act
d. 28-hour day

21. _____ is a concept in ethics with several meanings. It is often used synonymously with such concepts as responsibility, answerability, enforcement, blameworthiness, liability and other terms associated with the expectation of account-giving. As an aspect of governance, it has been central to discussions related to problems in both the public and private (corporation) worlds.
   a. Usury
   b. A Stake in the Outcome
   c. A4e
   d. Accountability

22. _____ has been described as the 'process of social influence in which one person can enlist the aid and support of others in the accomplishment of a common task'. A definition more inclusive of followers comes from Alan Keith of Genentech who said '_____ is ultimately about creating a way for people to contribute to making something extraordinary happen.'

_____ is one of the most salient aspects of the organizational context. However, defining _____ has been challenging.

   a. 1990 Clean Air Act
   b. 28-hour day
   c. Situational leadership
   d. Leadership

23. There are two types of _____ relationships: formal and informal. Informal relationships develop on their own between partners. Formal _____, on the other hand, refers to assigned relationships, often associated with organizational _____ programs designed to promote employee development or to assist at-risk children and youth.
   a. Human resource management system
   b. Fix it twice
   c. Real Property Administrator
   d. Mentoring

24. The _____ is a chart that had been created by Bruce Henderson for the Boston Consulting Group in 1970 to help corporations with analyzing their business units or product lines. This helps the company allocate resources and is used as an analytical tool in brand marketing, product management, strategic management, and portfolio analysis. _____

To use the chart, analysts plot a scatter graph to rank the business units (or products) on the basis of their relative market shares and growth rates.

Chapter 10. HUMAN RESOURCE SYSTEMS

a. BCG matrix
b. Marketing plan
c. Marketing strategy
d. Market segment

25. The _____ is a trilateral trade bloc in North America created by the governments of the United States, Canada, and Mexico. The agreement creating the trade bloc came into force on January 1, 1994. It superseded the Canada-United States Free Trade Agreement between the U.S. and Canada.

a. Trade union
b. Business war game
c. Career portfolios
d. North American Free Trade Agreement

26. _____ in its literal sense is the process of transformation of local or regional phenomena into global ones. It can be described as a process by which the people of the world are unified into a single society and function together.

This process is a combination of economic, technological, sociocultural and political forces.

a. Globalization
b. Histogram
c. Collaborative Planning, Forecasting and Replenishment
d. Cost Management

27. _____ is a method by which the job performance of an employee is evaluated _____ is a part of career development.

_____s are regular reviews of employee performance within organizations

Generally, the aims of a _____ are to:

- Give feedback on performance to employees.
- Identify employee training needs.
- Document criteria used to allocate organizational rewards.
- Form a basis for personnel decisions: salary increases, promotions, disciplinary actions, etc.
- Provide the opportunity for organizational diagnosis and development.
- Facilitate communication between employee and administraton
- Validate selection techniques and human resource policies to meet federal Equal Employment Opportunity requirements.

Chapter 10. HUMAN RESOURCE SYSTEMS

A common approach to assessing performance is to use a numerical or scalar rating system whereby managers are asked to score an individual against a number of objectives/attributes. In some companies, employees receive assessments from their manager, peers, subordinates and customers while also performing a self assessment.

   a. Performance appraisal
   b. Progressive discipline
   c. Human resource management
   d. Personnel management

28. A _____ is a set of categories designed to elicit information about a quantitative or a qualitative attribute. In the social sciences, common examples are the Likert scale and 1-10 _____s in which a person selects the number which is considered to reflect the perceived quality of a product.

A _____ is an instrument that requires the rater to assign the rated object that have numerals assigned to them.

   a. Polytomous Rasch model
   b. Spearman-Brown prediction formula
   c. Rating scale
   d. Thurstone scale

29. _____ is a term defined by the Oxford English Dictionary as an individual's 'course or progress through life '. It is usually considered to pertain to remunerative work (and sometimes also formal education.)

The etymology of the term is somewhat ironic in that it comes from the Latin word carrera, which means race .

   a. Spatial mismatch
   b. Career
   c. Career planning
   d. Nursing shortage

30. _____ is a subset of career management. _____ applies the concepts of Strategic planning and Marketing to taking charge of one's professional future.
   a. Military recruitment
   b. Forced retention
   c. TDY
   d. Career planning

Chapter 10. HUMAN RESOURCE SYSTEMS

31. _____ refers to the movement of cash into or out of a business or financial product. It is usually measured during a specified, finite period of time. Measurement of _____ can be used

- to determine a project's rate of return or value. The time of _____s into and out of projects are used as inputs in financial models such as internal rate of return, and net present value.
- to determine problems with a business's liquidity. Being profitable does not necessarily mean being liquid. A company can fail because of a shortage of cash, even while profitable.
- as an alternate measure of a business's profits when it is believed that accrual accounting concepts do not represent economic realities. For example, a company may be notionally profitable but generating little operational cash (as may be the case for a company that barters its products rather than selling for cash.) In such a case, the company may be deriving additional operating cash by issuing shares evaluating default risk, re-investment requirements, etc.

_____ is a generic term used differently depending on the context. It may be defined by users for their own purposes.

a. Gross profit margin
b. Gross profit
c. Sweat equity
d. Cash flow

32. _____ is a statistical term used in national accounts, Balance of Payments statistics and sometimes in corporate accounts as well. It refers basically to the total gross (pre-tax) wages paid by employers to employees for work done in an accounting period, such as a quarter or a year.

However, in reality, the aggregate includes more than just gross wages, at least in national accounts and balance of payments statistics.

a. 28-hour day
b. 33 Strategies of War
c. 1990 Clean Air Act
d. Compensation of employees

33. In a human resources context, _____ or labor _____ is the rate at which an employer gains and loses employees. Simple ways to describe it are 'how long employees tend to stay' or 'the rate of traffic through the revolving door.' _____ is measured for individual companies and for their industry as a whole. If an employer is said to have a high _____ relative to its competitors, it means that employees of that company have a shorter average tenure than those of other companies in the same industry.

Chapter 10. HUMAN RESOURCE SYSTEMS

a. Ten year occupational employment projection
b. Career portfolios
c. Continuous
d. Turnover

34. _____ is a broad concept including proper prioritizing between career and ambition on one hand, compared with pleasure, leisure, family and spiritual development on the other.

As the separation between work and home life has diminished, this concept has become more relevant than ever before.

The expression was first used in the late 1970s to describe the balance between an individual's work and personal life.

a. Workforce
b. Quality of working life
c. Division of labour
d. Work-life balance

35. _____ is a type of trade policy that allows traders to act and transact without interference from government. Thus, the policy permits trading partners mutual gains from trade, with goods and services produced according to the theory of comparative advantage.

Under a _____ policy, prices are a reflection of true supply and demand, and are the sole determinant of resource allocation.

a. 28-hour day
b. Free Trade
c. 1990 Clean Air Act
d. 33 Strategies of War

36. The _____ is a 1935 United States federal law that limits the means with which employers may react to workers in the private sector that organize labor unions, engage in collective bargaining, and take part in strikes and other forms of concerted activity in support of their demands. The Act does not, on the other hand, cover those workers who are covered by the Railway Labor Act, agricultural employees, domestic employees, supervisors, independent contractors and some close relatives of individual employers.

It was in a context of severe economic troubles that the Wagner Act came into effect.

a. National Labor Relations Act
b. 33 Strategies of War
c. 28-hour day
d. 1990 Clean Air Act

37. In organized labor, _____ is the method whereby workers organize together (usually in unions) to meet, converse, and negotiate upon the work conditions with their employers normally resulting in a written contract setting forth the wages, hours, and other conditions to be observed for a stipulated period. It is the practice in which union and company representatives meet to negotiate a new labor contract. In various national labor and employment law contexts, the term _____ takes on a more specific legal meaning. In a broad sense, however, it is the coming together of workers to negotiate their employment.
a. Paid time off
b. Labour law
c. Labor rights
d. Collective bargaining

Chapter 11. LEADING—TO INSPIRE EFFORT

1. _____ has been described as the 'process of social influence in which one person can enlist the aid and support of others in the accomplishment of a common task' . A definition more inclusive of followers comes from Alan Keith of Genentech who said '_____ is ultimately about creating a way for people to contribute to making something extraordinary happen.'

_____ is one of the most salient aspects of the organizational context. However, defining _____ has been challenging.

   a. Situational leadership
   b. Leadership
   c. 28-hour day
   d. 1990 Clean Air Act

2. _____ of the learning curve effect and the closely related experience curve effect express the relationship between equations for experience and efficiency or between efficiency gains and investment in the effort. The experience of 'learning curves' was first observed by the 19th Century German psychologist Hermann Ebbinghaus according to the difficulty of memorizing varying numbers of verbal stimuli, and subsequent learning about the complex processes of learning are discussed in the

.

The rule used for representing the learning curve effect states that the more times a task has been performed, the less time will be required on each subsequent iteration.

   a. Models
   b. Distribution
   c. Point biserial correlation coefficient
   d. Spatial Decision Support Systems

3. Contingency leadership theory in organizational studies is a type of leadership theory, leadership style, and leadership model that presumes that different leadership styles are contingent to different situations. It is also referred as _____ ® theory although, as originally convened, the situational theory term is much more restrictive. The original situational theory argues that the best type of leadership is totally determined by the situational variables. Currently there are many styles of leadership.
   a. Situational leadership
   b. Situational theory
   c. 28-hour day
   d. 1990 Clean Air Act

Chapter 11. LEADING—TO INSPIRE EFFORT

4. The _____ is a leadership theory in the field of organizational studies developed by Robert House in 1971 and revised in 1996. The theory that a leader's behavior is contingent to the satisfaction, motivation and performance of subordinates. The revised version also argues that the leader engage in behaviors that complement subordinate's abilities and compensate for deficiencies.
   a. Path-goal theory
   b. Human relations
   c. Corporate Culture
   d. Sociotechnical systems

5. _____ is a term used to classify a group leadership theories that inquire the interactions between leaders and followers. A transactional leader focuses more on a series of 'transactions'. This person is interested in looking out for oneself, having exchange benefits with their subordinates and clarify a sense of duty with rewards and punishments to reach goals.
   a. 28-hour day
   b. Transactional leadership
   c. 1990 Clean Air Act
   d. 33 Strategies of War

6. _____ is a leadership style that defines as leadership that creates voluble and positive change in the followers. A transformational leader focuses on 'transforming' others to help each other, to look out for each other, be encouraging, harmonious, and look out for the organization as a whole. In this leadership, the leader enhances the motivation, moral and performance of his follower group.
   a. Strong-Campbell Interest Inventory
   b. Polynomial conjoint measurement
   c. SESAMO
   d. Transformational leadership

7. _____ , often measured as an _____ Quotient (EQ), is a term that describes the ability, capacity, skill or (in the case of the trait _____ model) a self-perceived ability, to identify, assess, and manage the emotions of one's self, of others, and of groups. Different models have been proposed for the definition of _____ and disagreement exists as to how the term should be used. Despite these disagreements, which are often highly technical, the ability _____ and trait _____ models (but not the mixed models) are enjoying considerable support in the literature and have successful applications in many different domains.
   a. Emotional intelligence
   b. AAAI
   c. A Stake in the Outcome
   d. A4e

8. _____ was a writer, management consultant, and self-described 'social ecologist.' Widely considered to be 'the father of modern management,' his 39 books and countless scholarly and popular articles explored how humans are organized across all sectors of society--in business, government and the nonprofit world. His writings have predicted many of the major developments of the late twentieth century, including privatization and decentralization; the rise of Japan to economic world power; the decisive importance of marketing; and the emergence of the information society with its necessity of lifelong learning. In 1959, Drucker coined the term 'knowledge worker' and later in his life considered knowledge work productivity to be the next frontier of management.
   a. Debora L. Spar
   b. Jacques Al-Salawat Nasruddin Nasser
   c. Peter Ferdinand Drucker
   d. Chrissie Hynde

Chapter 12. MOTIVATION AND JOB DESIGN

1. _____ is a term that was popularized by renowned psychologist David McClelland in 1961. However, it should be recognized that McClellend's thinking was strongly influenced by the pioneering work of Henry Murray who first identified underlying psychological human needs and motivational processes (1938.) It was Murray who set out a taxonomy of needs, including Achievement, Power and Affiliation - and placed these in the context of an integrated motivational model.

   a. 1990 Clean Air Act
   b. Need for Achievement
   c. Two-factor theory
   d. Need for Power

2. _____ was developed by Frederick Herzberg, a psychologist who found that job satisfaction and job dissatisfaction acted independently of each other. _____ states that there are certain factors in the workplace that cause job satisfaction, while a separate set of factors cause dissatisfaction.

   a. Need for power
   b. 1990 Clean Air Act
   c. Need for Achievement
   d. Two-factor theory

3. _____ are job factors that can cause dissatisfaction if missing but do not necessarily motivate employees if increased.

   _____ have mostly to do with the job environment. These factors are important or notable only when they are lacking.

   a. Work system
   b. Work-at-home scheme
   c. Split shift
   d. Hygiene factors

4. In law, _____ is the term to describe a partnership between two or more parties.

In England a number of statutes on the subject have been passed, the chief being the Bastardy Act of 1845, and the Bastardy Laws Amendment Acts of 1872 and 1873. The mother of a bastard may summon the putative father to petty sessions within twelve months of the birth (or at any later time if he is proved to have contributed to the child's support within twelve months after the birth), and the justices, as after hearing evidence on both sides, may, if the mother's evidence be corroborated in some material particular, adjudge the man to be the putative father of the child, and order him to pay a sum not exceeding five shillings a week for its maintenance, together with a sum for expenses incidental to the birth, or the funeral expenses, if it has died before the date of order, and the costs of the proceedings.

Chapter 12. MOTIVATION AND JOB DESIGN

a. Adam Smith
b. Abraham Harold Maslow
c. Affiliation
d. Affirmative action

5. _____ refers to an individual's desire for significant accomplishment, mastering of skills, control, or high standards. The term was introduced by the psychologist, David McClelland.

_____ is related to the difficulty of tasks people choose to undertake.

a. 1990 Clean Air Act
b. Need for Achievement
c. Need for power
d. Two-factor theory

6. The _____ is a term that was popularised by David McClelland and describes a person's need to feel a sense of involvement and 'belonging' within a social group. However, it should be recognised that McClellend's thinking was strongly influenced by the pioneering work of Henry Murray who first identified underlying psychological human needs and motivational processes (1938.) It was Murray who set out a taxonomy of needs, including Achievement, Power and Affiliation - and placed these in the context of an integrated motivational model.
a. Polynomial conjoint measurement
b. SESAMO
c. Strong-Campbell Interest Inventory
d. Need for Affiliation

7. The _____ is a monograph published by Frederick Winslow Taylor in 1911. This influential monograph is the basis of modern organization and decision theory and has motivated administrators and students of managerial technique. Taylor was an American mechanical engineer and a management consultant in his later years.
a. 28-hour day
b. 1990 Clean Air Act
c. Principles of Scientific Management
d. 33 Strategies of War

8. _____ is a theory of management that analyzes and synthesizes workflows, with the objective of improving labour productivity. The core ideas of the theory were developed by Frederick Winslow Taylor in the 1880s and 1890s, and were first published in his monographs, Shop Management and The Principles of _____ Taylor believed that decisions based upon tradition and rules of thumb should be replaced by precise procedures developed after careful study of an individual at work.

Chapter 12. MOTIVATION AND JOB DESIGN

a. Master production schedule
b. Value engineering
c. Capacity planning
d. Scientific Management

9. The _____ 1970 is an Act of the United Kingdom Parliament which prohibits any less favourable treatment between men and women in terms of pay and conditions of employment. It came into force on 29 December 1975. The term pay is interpreted in a broad sense to include, on top of wages, things like holidays, pension rights, company perks and some kinds of bonuses.
   a. Oncale v. Sundowner Offshore Services
   b. Architectural Barriers Act of 1968
   c. Australian labour law
   d. Equal Pay Act

10. The _____, Pub. L. No. 88-38, 77 Stat. 56, (June 10, 1963) codified at 29 U.S.C. Â§ 206(d), is a United States federal law amending the Fair Labor Standards Act, aimed at abolishing wage differentials based on sex. In passing the bill, Congress denounces sex discrimination.
    a. Extra time
    b. Architectural Barriers Act of 1968
    c. Invitee
    d. Equal Pay Act of 1963

11. _____ attempts to explain relational satisfaction in terms of perceptions of fair/unfair distributions of resources within interpersonal relationships. _____ is considered as one of the justice theories, It was first developed in 1962 by John Stacey Adams, a workplace and behavioral psychologist, who asserted that employees seek to maintain equity between the inputs that they bring to a job and the outcomes that they receive from it against the perceived inputs and outcomes of others (Adams, 1965.) The belief is that people value fair treatment which causes them to be motivated to keep the fairness maintained within the relationships of their co-workers and the organization.
    a. A4e
    b. AAAI
    c. A Stake in the Outcome
    d. Equity theory

12. _____ is about the mental processes regarding choice, or choosing. It explains the processes that an individual undergoes to make choices. In organizational behavior study, _____ is a motivation theory first proposed by Victor Vroom of the Yale School of Management.

a. AAAI
b. A Stake in the Outcome
c. A4e
d. Expectancy theory

13. _____ of the learning curve effect and the closely related experience curve effect express the relationship between equations for experience and efficiency or between efficiency gains and investment in the effort. The experience of 'learning curves' was first observed by the 19th Century German psychologist Hermann Ebbinghaus according to the difficulty of memorizing varying numbers of verbal stimuli, and subsequent learning about the complex processes of learning are discussed in the

.

The rule used for representing the learning curve effect states that the more times a task has been performed, the less time will be required on each subsequent iteration.

a. Point biserial correlation coefficient
b. Spatial Decision Support Systems
c. Distribution
d. Models

14. _____ is a process of agreeing upon objectives within an organization so that management and employees agree to the objectives and understand what they are in the organization.

The term '_____' was first popularized by Peter Drucker in his 1954 book 'The Practice of Management'.

The essence of _____ is participative goal setting, choosing course of actions and decision making.

a. Clean sheet review
b. Job enrichment
c. Business economics
d. Management by objectives

15. _____ is the use of empirically demonstrated behavior change techniques to improve behavior, such as altering an individual's behaviors and reactions to stimuli through positive and negative reinforcement of adaptive behavior and/or the reduction of maladaptive behavior through punishment and/or therapy.

The first use of the term _____ appears to have been by Edward Thorndike in 1911

Chapter 12. MOTIVATION AND JOB DESIGN

a. 28-hour day
b. 1990 Clean Air Act
c. 33 Strategies of War
d. Behavior modification

16. _____ refers to training in different ways to improve overall performance. It takes advantage of the particular effectiveness of each training method, while at the same time attempting to neglect the shortcomings of that method by combining it with other methods that address its weaknesses.

Cross training is employee-employer field means, training employees to do one another's work.

a. 28-hour day
b. 1990 Clean Air Act
c. 33 Strategies of War
d. Cross-training

17. _____ is the use of consequences to modify the occurrence and form of behavior. _____ is distinguished from classical conditioning (also called respondent conditioning, or Pavlovian conditioning) in that _____ deals with the modification of 'voluntary behavior' or operant behavior. Operant behavior 'operates' on the environment and is maintained by its consequences, while classical conditioning deals with the conditioning of respondent behaviors which are elicited by antecedent conditions.
   a. Unemployment insurance
   b. Occupational Safety and Health Administration
   c. Outsourcing
   d. Operant conditioning

18. In operant conditioning, _____ occurs when an event following a response causes an increase in the probability of that response occurring in the future. Response strength can be assessed by measures such as the frequency with which the response is made (for example, a pigeon may peck a key more times in the session), or the speed with which it is made (for example, a rat may run a maze faster.) The environment change contingent upon the response is called a reinforcer.
   a. Meetings, Incentives, Conferences, and Exhibitions
   b. Reinforcement
   c. Historiometry
   d. Diminishing Manufacturing Sources and Material Shortages

Chapter 12. MOTIVATION AND JOB DESIGN

19. _____ refers to the movement of cash into or out of a business or financial product. It is usually measured during a specified, finite period of time. Measurement of _____ can be used

- to determine a project's rate of return or value. The time of _____s into and out of projects are used as inputs in financial models such as internal rate of return, and net present value.
- to determine problems with a business's liquidity. Being profitable does not necessarily mean being liquid. A company can fail because of a shortage of cash, even while profitable.
- as an alternate measure of a business's profits when it is believed that accrual accounting concepts do not represent economic realities. For example, a company may be notionally profitable but generating little operational cash (as may be the case for a company that barters its products rather than selling for cash.) In such a case, the company may be deriving additional operating cash by issuing shares evaluating default risk, re-investment requirements, etc.

_____ is a generic term used differently depending on the context. It may be defined by users for their own purposes.

   a. Cash flow
   b. Sweat equity
   c. Gross profit margin
   d. Gross profit

20. _____ can be considered to have three main components: quality control, quality assurance and quality improvement. _____ is focused not only on product quality, but also the means to achieve it. _____ therefore uses quality assurance and control of processes as well as products to achieve more consistent quality.
   a. 28-hour day
   b. Quality management
   c. Total quality management
   d. 1990 Clean Air Act

21. _____ is a business management strategy aimed at embedding awareness of quality in all organizational processes. _____ has been widely used in manufacturing, education, hospitals, call centers, government, and service industries, as well as NASA space and science programs.

As defined by the International Organization for Standardization (ISO):

> '_____ is a management approach for an organization, centered on quality, based on the participation of all its members and aiming at long-term success through customer satisfaction, and benefits to all members of the organization and to society.' ISO 8402:1994

One major aim is to reduce variation from every process so that greater consistency of effort is obtained. (Royse, D., Thyer, B., Padgett D., ' Logan T., 2006)

a. 28-hour day
b. Total quality management
c. Quality management
d. 1990 Clean Air Act

22. _____ is an advertisement in which a particular product specifically mentions a competitor by name for the express purpose of showing why the competitor is inferior to the product naming it.

This should not be confused with parody advertisements, where a fictional product is being advertised for the purpose of poking fun at the particular advertisement, nor should it be confused with the use of a coined brand name for the purpose of comparing the product without actually naming an actual competitor. ('Wikipedia tastes better and is less filling than the Encyclopedia Galactica.')

In the 1980s, during what has been referred to as the cola wars, soft-drink manufacturer Pepsi ran a series of advertisements where people, caught on hidden camera, in a blind taste test, chose Pepsi over rival Coca-Cola.

a. 33 Strategies of War
b. 28-hour day
c. 1990 Clean Air Act
d. Comparative advertising

23. Procter is a surname, and may also refer to:

- Bryan Waller Procter (pseud. Barry Cornwall), English poet
- Goodwin Procter, American law firm
- _____, consumer products multinational

a. Downstream
b. Master and Servant Acts
c. Strict liability
d. Procter ' Gamble

24. In organizational development (OD), _____ is the application of Socio-Technical Systems principles and techniques to the humanization of work.

The aims of _____ to improved job satisfaction, to improved through-put, to improved quality and to reduced employee problems, e.g., grievances, absenteeism.

Chapter 12. MOTIVATION AND JOB DESIGN

Under scientific management people would be directed by reason and the problems of industrial unrest would be appropriately (i.e., scientifically) addressed.

a. Management process
b. Path-goal theory
c. Graduate recruitment
d. Work design

25. _____ describes how content an individual is with his or her job.

The happier people are within their job, the more satisfied they are said to be. _____ is not the same as motivation, although it is clearly linked.

a. Human relations
b. Job satisfaction
c. Goal-setting theory
d. Job analysis

26. _____ refers to metrics and measures of output from production processes, per unit of input. Labor _____, for example, is typically measured as a ratio of output per labor-hour, an input. _____ may be conceived of as a metrics of the technical or engineering efficiency of production.
a. Master production schedule
b. Productivity
c. Remanufacturing
d. Value engineering

27. _____ refers to the difference between the cost of materials purchased by a company plus the cost of the labor to assemble a product and the price at which the company sells the product. An example is the price of gasoline at the pump over the price of the oil in it. In national accounts used in macroeconomics, it refers to the contribution of the factors of production, i.e., land, labor, and capital goods, to raising the value of a product and corresponds to the incomes received by the owners of these factors.
a. Deregulation
b. Rehn-Meidner Model
c. Value added
d. Minimum wage

Chapter 12. MOTIVATION AND JOB DESIGN

28. _____ is the use of control systems (such as numerical control, programmable logic control, and other industrial control systems), in concert with other applications of information technology (such as computer-aided technologies [CAD, CAM, CAx]), to control industrial machinery and processes, reducing the need for human intervention. In the scope of industrialization, _____ is a step beyond mechanization. Whereas mechanization provided human operators with machinery to assist them with the physical requirements of work, _____ greatly reduces the need for human sensory and mental requirements as well.

a. A Stake in the Outcome
b. A4e
c. AAAI
d. Automation

29. _____ means increasing the scope of a job through extending the range of its job duties and responsibilities. This contradicts the principles of specialisation and the division of labour whereby work is divided into small units, each of which is performed repetitively by an individual worker. Some motivational theories suggest that the boredom and alienation caused by the division of labour can actually cause efficiency to fall.

a. Job enlargement
b. Mock interview
c. Delayering
d. Centralization

30. _____ is an attempt to motivate employees by giving them the opportunity to use the range of their abilities. It is an idea that was developed by the American psychologist Frederick Herzberg in the 1950s. It can be contrasted to job enlargement which simply increases the number of tasks without changing the challenge.

a. C-A-K-E
b. Catfish effect
c. Cash cow
d. Job enrichment

31. _____ is an approach to management development where an individual is moved through a schedule of assignments designed to give him or her a breadth of exposure to the entire operation.

_____ is also practiced to allow qualified employees to gain more insights into the processes of a company, and to reduce boredom and increase job satisfaction through job variation.

The term _____ can also mean the scheduled exchange of persons in offices, especially in public offices, prior to the end of incumbency or the legislative period.

a. 28-hour day
b. 33 Strategies of War
c. 1990 Clean Air Act
d. Job rotation

32. In mathematical logic, _____ is a valid argument and rule of inference which makes the inference that, if the conjunction A and B is true, then A is true, and B is true.

In formal language:

$$A \wedge B \vdash A$$

or

$$A \wedge B \vdash B$$

The argument has one premise, namely a conjunction, and one often uses _____ in longer arguments to derive one of the conjuncts.

An example in English:

It's raining and it's pouring.

a. 1990 Clean Air Act
b. Validity
c. Fuzzy logic
d. Simplification

33. _____ is one of the managerial functions like planning, organizing, staffing and directing. It is an important function because it helps to check the errors and to take the corrective action so that deviation from standards are minimized and stated goals of the organization are achieved in desired manner.According to modern concepts, _____ is a foreseeing action whereas earlier concept of _____ was used only when errors were detected. _____ in management means setting standards, measuring actual performance and taking corrective action.
a. Schedule of reinforcement
b. Turnover
c. Control
d. Decision tree pruning

Chapter 12. MOTIVATION AND JOB DESIGN

34. The legal _____ varies from nation to nation. The weekend is a part of the week usually lasting one or two days in which most paid workers do not work.

In Muslim-majority countries the legal work week in the Middle East is typically either Saturday through Wednesday, Saturday through Thursday or Sunday through Thursday as in Egypt.

a. Workweek
b. Day One Christian Ministries
c. Business day
d. Working Time Directive

35. _____, e-commuting, e-work, telework, working from home (WFH), or working at home (WAH) is a work arrangement in which employees enjoy flexibility in working location and hours. In other words, the daily commute to a central place of work is replaced by telecommunication links. Many work from home, while others, occasionally also referred to as nomad workers or web commuters utilize mobile telecommunications technology to work from coffee shops or myriad other locations.

a. 28-hour day
b. 33 Strategies of War
c. 1990 Clean Air Act
d. Telecommuting

36. _____ is a broad label that refers to any individuals or households that use goods and services generated within the economy. The concept of a _____ is used in different contexts, so that the usage and significance of the term may vary.

Typically when business people and economists talk of _____s they are talking about person as _____, an aggregated commodity item with little individuality other than that expressed in the buy/not-buy decision.

a. 33 Strategies of War
b. Consumer
c. 28-hour day
d. 1990 Clean Air Act

37. The _____ was enacted in 1972 by the United States Congress. It established the United States Consumer Product Safety Commission as an independent agency of the United States federal government and defined its basic authority. The act gives CPSC the power to develop safety standards and pursue recalls for products that present unreasonable or substantial risks of injury or death to consumers.

a. Consumer Product Safety Act
b. 1990 Clean Air Act
c. 28-hour day
d. 33 Strategies of War

38. An _____ is a natural person, business, or corporation which provides goods or services to another entity under terms specified in a contract or within a verbal agreement. Unlike an employee, an _____ does not work regularly for an employer but works as and when required, during which time she or he may be subject to the Law of Agency. _____s are usually paid on a freelance basis.
a. Occupational Safety and Health Act
b. Equal Pay Act of 1963
c. Independent contractor
d. Employment protection legislation

Chapter 13. TEAMS AND TEAMWORK

1. _____, widely known as F. W. Taylor, was an American mechanical engineer who sought to improve industrial efficiency. He is regarded as the father of scientific management, and was one of the first management consultants.

Taylor was one of the intellectual leaders of the Efficiency Movement and his ideas, broadly conceived, were highly influential in the Progressive Era.

   a. Douglas N. Daft
   b. Geoffrey Colvin
   c. Jonah Jacob Goldberg
   d. Frederick Winslow Taylor

2. _____ is a concept in ethics with several meanings. It is often used synonymously with such concepts as responsibility, answerability, enforcement, blameworthiness, liability and other terms associated with the expectation of account-giving. As an aspect of governance, it has been central to discussions related to problems in both the public and private (corporation) worlds.
   a. A4e
   b. Accountability
   c. Usury
   d. A Stake in the Outcome

3. In the social psychology of groups, _____ is the phenomenon of people making less effort to achieve a goal when they work in a group than when they work alone. This is seen as one of the main reasons groups are sometimes less productive than the combined performance of their members working as individuals.

   • Ringelmann, Max : 1913

Research began in 1913 with Max Ringelmann's study. He found that when he asked a group of men to pull on a rope, that they did not pull as hard, or put as much effort into the activity, as they did when they were pulling alone.

   a. Machiavellianism
   b. Personal space
   c. Social loafing
   d. Self-enhancement

4. A _____ is a group of employees from various functional areas of the organization - research, engineering, marketing, finance. human resources, and operations, for example - who are all focused on a specific objective and are responsible to work as a team to improve coordination and innovation across divisions and resolve mutual problems.

Chapter 13. TEAMS AND TEAMWORK

a. Sociotechnical systems
b. Goal-setting theory
c. Cross-functional team
d. Graduate recruitment

5. A _____ is a volunteer group composed of workers (or even students), usually under the leadership of their supervisor (but they can elect a team leader), who are trained to identify, analyse and solve work-related problems and present their solutions to management in order to improve the performance of the organization, and motivate and enrich the work of employees. When matured, true _____s become self-managing, having gained the confidence of management. _____s are an alternative to the dehumanising concept of the Division of Labour, where workers or individuals are treated like robots.
a. Quality circle
b. Competency-based job descriptions
c. Certified in Production and Inventory Management
d. Connectionist expert systems

6. _____ can be considered to have three main components: quality control, quality assurance and quality improvement. _____ is focused not only on product quality, but also the means to achieve it. _____ therefore uses quality assurance and control of processes as well as products to achieve more consistent quality.
a. Quality management
b. 28-hour day
c. Total quality management
d. 1990 Clean Air Act

7. _____ is a business management strategy aimed at embedding awareness of quality in all organizational processes. _____ has been widely used in manufacturing, education, hospitals, call centers, government, and service industries, as well as NASA space and science programs.

As defined by the International Organization for Standardization (ISO):

'_____ is a management approach for an organization, centered on quality, based on the participation of all its members and aiming at long-term success through customer satisfaction, and benefits to all members of the organization and to society.' ISO 8402:1994

One major aim is to reduce variation from every process so that greater consistency of effort is obtained. (Royse, D., Thyer, B., Padgett D., ' Logan T., 2006)

Chapter 13. TEAMS AND TEAMWORK

a. Quality management
b. Total quality management
c. 28-hour day
d. 1990 Clean Air Act

8. The U.S. _____ is an independent agency of the United States government which holds primary responsibility for enforcing the federal securities laws and regulating the securities industry, the nation's stock and options exchanges, and other electronic securities markets. The SEC was created by section 4 of the Securities Exchange Act of 1934 (now codified as 15 U.S.C. § 78d and commonly referred to as the 1934 Act.)

a. 28-hour day
b. 1990 Clean Air Act
c. 33 Strategies of War
d. Securities and Exchange Commission

9. A _____ -- also known as a geographically dispersed team -- is a group of individuals who work across time, space, and organizational boundaries with links strengthened by webs of communication technology. They have complementary skills and are committed to a common purpose, have interdependent performance goals, and share an approach to work for which they hold themselves mutually accountable. Geographically dispersed teams allow organizations to hire and retain the best people regardless of location.

a. Trademark
b. Virtual team
c. Kanban
d. Risk management

10. _____ is a civil designation for persons who are incorporated in a fixed or permanent way to a society or group: regular member of the working staff, permanent staff distinguished from a supernumerary.

The term '_____' and its counterpart, 'supernumerary,' originated in Spanish and Latin American academy and government; it is now also used in countries all over the world, such as France, the U.S., England, Italy, etc.

There are _____ members of surgical organizations, of universities, of gastronomical associations, etc.

a. Abraham Harold Maslow
b. Adam Smith
c. Numerary
d. Affiliation

11. _____ has been described as the 'process of social influence in which one person can enlist the aid and support of others in the accomplishment of a common task'. A definition more inclusive of followers comes from Alan Keith of Genentech who said '_____ is ultimately about creating a way for people to contribute to making something extraordinary happen.'

_____ is one of the most salient aspects of the organizational context. However, defining _____ has been challenging.

   a. Situational leadership
   b. 1990 Clean Air Act
   c. Leadership
   d. 28-hour day

12. _____ can be regarded as an outcome of mental processes (cognitive process) leading to the selection of a course of action among several alternatives. Every _____ process produces a final choice. The output can be an action or an opinion of choice.
   a. Decision making
   b. 33 Strategies of War
   c. 1990 Clean Air Act
   d. 28-hour day

13. _____ is a type of thought exhibited by group members who try to minimize conflict and reach consensus without critically testing, analyzing, and evaluating ideas. Individual creativity, uniqueness, and independent thinking are lost in the pursuit of group cohesiveness, as are the advantages of reasonable balance in choice and thought that might normally be obtained by making decisions as a group. During _____, members of the group avoid promoting viewpoints outside the comfort zone of consensus thinking.
   a. Psychological statistics
   b. Diffusion of responsibility
   c. Self-report inventory
   d. Groupthink

Chapter 14. COMMUNICATION AND INTERPERSONAL SKILLS

1. _____ has been described as the 'process of social influence in which one person can enlist the aid and support of others in the accomplishment of a common task' . A definition more inclusive of followers comes from Alan Keith of Genentech who said '_____ is ultimately about creating a way for people to contribute to making something extraordinary happen.'

_____ is one of the most salient aspects of the organizational context. However, defining _____ has been challenging.

   a. Leadership
   b. Situational leadership
   c. 28-hour day
   d. 1990 Clean Air Act

2. Business-to-consumer describes activities of businesses serving end consumers with products and/or services.

An example of a _____ transaction would be a person buying a pair of shoes from a retailer. The transactions that led to the shoes being available for purchase, that is the purchase of the leather, laces, rubber, etc.

   a. Market environment
   b. Green marketing
   c. PEST analysis
   d. B2C

3. _____ occurs when expectant women are fired, not hired, or otherwise discriminated against due to their pregnancy or intention to become pregnant. Common forms of _____ include not being hired due to visible pregnancy or likelihood of becoming pregnant, being fired after informing an employer of one's pregnancy, being fired after maternity leave, and receiving a pay dock due to pregnancy. In the United States, since 1978, employers are legally bound to provide what insurance, leave pay, and additional support that would be bestowed upon any employee with medical leave or disability.
   a. 1990 Clean Air Act
   b. 33 Strategies of War
   c. 28-hour day
   d. Pregnancy Discrimination

4. The _____ refers to a cognitive bias whereby the perception of a particular trait is influenced by the perception of the former traits in a sequence of interpretations.

Edward L. Thorndike was the first to support the _____ with empirical research. In a psychology study published in 1920, Thorndike asked commanding officers to rate their soldiers; Thorndike found high cross-correlation between all positive and all negative traits.

a. Sunk costs
b. Distinction bias
c. Cognitive biases
d. Halo effect

5. _____ refers to the movement of cash into or out of a business or financial product. It is usually measured during a specified, finite period of time. Measurement of _____ can be used

- to determine a project's rate of return or value. The time of _____s into and out of projects are used as inputs in financial models such as internal rate of return, and net present value.
- to determine problems with a business's liquidity. Being profitable does not necessarily mean being liquid. A company can fail because of a shortage of cash, even while profitable.
- as an alternate measure of a business's profits when it is believed that accrual accounting concepts do not represent economic realities. For example, a company may be notionally profitable but generating little operational cash (as may be the case for a company that barters its products rather than selling for cash.) In such a case, the company may be deriving additional operating cash by issuing shares evaluating default risk, re-investment requirements, etc.

_____ is a generic term used differently depending on the context. It may be defined by users for their own purposes.

a. Gross profit
b. Sweat equity
c. Gross profit margin
d. Cash flow

6. The U.S. _____ is an independent agency of the United States government which holds primary responsibility for enforcing the federal securities laws and regulating the securities industry, the nation's stock and options exchanges, and other electronic securities markets. The SEC was created by section 4 of the Securities Exchange Act of 1934 (now codified as 15 U.S.C. § 78d and commonly referred to as the 1934 Act.)
a. 33 Strategies of War
b. 1990 Clean Air Act
c. 28-hour day
d. Securities and Exchange Commission

7. _____ describes the situation when output from (or information about the result of) an event or phenomenon in the past will influence the same event/phenomenon in the present or future. When an event is part of a chain of cause-and-effect that forms a circuit or loop, then the event is said to 'feed back' into itself.

Chapter 14. COMMUNICATION AND INTERPERSONAL SKILLS

_____ is also a synonym for:

- _____ signal; the information about the initial event that is the basis for subsequent modification of the event.
- _____ loop; the causal path that leads from the initial generation of the _____ signal to the subsequent modification of the event.

_____ is a mechanism, process or signal that is looped back to control a system within itself. Such a loop is called a _____ loop.

a. Feedback
b. Positive feedback
c. 1990 Clean Air Act
d. Feedback loop

8. _____ in its literal sense is the process of transformation of local or regional phenomena into global ones. It can be described as a process by which the people of the world are unified into a single society and function together.

This process is a combination of economic, technological, sociocultural and political forces.

a. Cost Management
b. Histogram
c. Collaborative Planning, Forecasting and Replenishment
d. Globalization

9. A _____ is a subset of the overall internal controls of a business covering the application of people, documents, technologies, and procedures by management accountants to solving business problems such as costing a product, service or a business-wide strategy. _____s are distinct from regular information systems in that they are used to analyze other information systems applied in operational activities in the organization. Academically, the term is commonly used to refer to the group of information management methods tied to the automation or support of human decision making, e.g. Decision Support Systems, Expert systems, and Executive information systems.

a. Strategic information system
b. 28-hour day
c. Management information system
d. 1990 Clean Air Act

10. The term _____ was introduced by anthropologist Edward T. Hall in 1966 to describe set measurable distances between people as they interact. The effects of _____, according to Hall, can be summarized by the following loose rule:

Chapter 14. COMMUNICATION AND INTERPERSONAL SKILLS

According to Jonathon Tabor distance-spacing theories based on the early animal-like human of German zoologist Heini Hediger, as found in his 1955 book Studies of the Behavior of Captive Animals in Zoos and Circuses. Hediger, in animals, had distinguished between flight distance , critical distance (attack boundary), personal distance (distance separating members of non-contact species, as a pair of swans), and social distance (intraspecies communication distance.)

   a. Proxemics
   b. 1990 Clean Air Act
   c. 28-hour day
   d. 33 Strategies of War

11. _____ refers to the long-term management of intractable conflicts. It is the label for the variety of ways by which people handle grievances--standing up for what they consider to be right and against what they consider to be wrong. Those ways include such diverse phenomena as gossip, ridicule, lynching, terrorism, warfare, feuding, genocide, law, mediation, and avoidance.
   a. 28-hour day
   b. 1990 Clean Air Act
   c. 33 Strategies of War
   d. Conflict management

12. _____ is a term that was popularized by renowned psychologist David McClelland in 1961. However, it should be recognized that McClellend's thinking was strongly influenced by the pioneering work of Henry Murray who first identified underlying psychological human needs and motivational processes (1938.) It was Murray who set out a taxonomy of needs, including Achievement, Power and Affiliation - and placed these in the context of an integrated motivational model.
   a. Need for Achievement
   b. Need for Power
   c. 1990 Clean Air Act
   d. Two-factor theory

13. _____ is a recursive process where two or more people or organizations work together in an intersection of common goals -- for example, an intellectual endeavor that is creative in nature--by sharing knowledge, learning and building consensus. _____ does not require leadership and can sometimes bring better results through decentralization and egalitarianism. In particular, teams that work collaboratively can obtain greater resources, recognition and reward when facing competition for finite resources. _____ is also present in opposing goals exhibiting the notion of adversarial _____, though this is not a common case for using the term.

a. 1990 Clean Air Act
b. Collectivism
c. 28-hour day
d. Collaboration

14. _____, a form of alternative dispute resolution (ADR), is a legal technique for the resolution of disputes outside the courts, wherein the parties to a dispute refer it to one or more persons (the 'arbitrators', 'arbiters' or 'arbitral tribunal'), by whose decision (the 'award') they agree to be bound. It is a settlement technique in which a third party reviews the case and imposes a decision that is legally binding for both sides. Other forms of ADR include mediation (a form of settlement negotiation facilitated by a neutral third party) and non-binding resolution by experts.
    a. A4e
    b. AAAI
    c. A Stake in the Outcome
    d. Arbitration

15. _____, a form of alternative dispute resolution (ADR) or 'appropriate dispute resolution', aims to assist two (or more) disputants in reaching an agreement. The parties themselves determine the conditions of any settlements reached-- rather than accepting something imposed by a third party. The disputes may involve (as parties) states, organizations, communities, individuals or other representatives with a vested interest in the outcome.
    a. Maximum medical improvement
    b. Meritor Savings Bank v. Vinson
    c. Foreign Corrupt Practices Act
    d. Mediation

Chapter 15. CHANGE LEADERSHIP AND STRESS

1. A _____ is the term given to a company that facilitates the learning of its members and continuously transforms itself. _____s develop as a result of the pressures facing modern organizations and enables them to remain competitive in the business environment. A _____ has five main features; systems thinking, personal mastery, mental models, shared vision and team learning.
   a. Quality function deployment
   b. Learning organization
   c. 1990 Clean Air Act
   d. Hoshin Kanri

2. _____ is an area of knowledge within organizational theory that studies models and theories about the way an organization learns and adapts.

In Organizational development (OD), learning is a characteristic of an adaptive organization, i.e., an organization that is able to sense changes in signals from its environment (both internal and external) and adapt accordingly.

   a. A Stake in the Outcome
   b. A4e
   c. AAAI
   d. Organizational learning

3. In human resources or industrial/organizational psychology, _____,' 'multisource feedback,' or 'multisource assessment,' is feedback that comes from all around an employee. '360' refers to the 360 degrees in a circle, with an individual figuratively in the center of the circle. Feedback is provided by subordinates, peers, and supervisors.
   a. Job knowledge
   b. Revolving door syndrome
   c. Personnel management
   d. 360-degree feedback

4. Business-to-consumer describes activities of businesses serving end consumers with products and/or services.

An example of a _____ transaction would be a person buying a pair of shoes from a retailer. The transactions that led to the shoes being available for purchase, that is the purchase of the leather, laces, rubber, etc.

   a. Green marketing
   b. B2C
   c. Market environment
   d. PEST analysis

Chapter 15. CHANGE LEADERSHIP AND STRESS

5. _____ was a writer, management consultant, and self-described 'social ecologist.' Widely considered to be 'the father of modern management,' his 39 books and countless scholarly and popular articles explored how humans are organized across all sectors of society--in business, government and the nonprofit world. His writings have predicted many of the major developments of the late twentieth century, including privatization and decentralization; the rise of Japan to economic world power; the decisive importance of marketing; and the emergence of the information society with its necessity of lifelong learning. In 1959, Drucker coined the term 'knowledge worker' and later in his life considered knowledge work productivity to be the next frontier of management.
   a. Chrissie Hynde
   b. Debora L. Spar
   c. Jacques Al-Salawat Nasruddin Nasser
   d. Peter Ferdinand Drucker

6. _____ describes the situation when output from (or information about the result of) an event or phenomenon in the past will influence the same event/phenomenon in the present or future. When an event is part of a chain of cause-and-effect that forms a circuit or loop, then the event is said to 'feed back' into itself.

_____ is also a synonym for:

- _____ signal; the information about the initial event that is the basis for subsequent modification of the event.
- _____ loop; the causal path that leads from the initial generation of the _____ signal to the subsequent modification of the event.

_____ is a mechanism, process or signal that is looped back to control a system within itself. Such a loop is called a _____ loop.

   a. Feedback
   b. Feedback loop
   c. 1990 Clean Air Act
   d. Positive feedback

7. _____ is the practice of using entrepreneurial skills without taking on the risks or accountability associated with entrepreneurial activities. It is practiced by employees within an established organization using a business model. Employees, perhaps engaged in a special project within a larger firm are supposed to behave as entrepreneurs, even though they have the resources and capabilities of the larger firm to draw upon.
   a. AAAI
   b. A4e
   c. A Stake in the Outcome
   d. Intrapreneurship

Chapter 15. CHANGE LEADERSHIP AND STRESS

8. _____, widely known as F. W. Taylor, was an American mechanical engineer who sought to improve industrial efficiency. He is regarded as the father of scientific management, and was one of the first management consultants.

Taylor was one of the intellectual leaders of the Efficiency Movement and his ideas, broadly conceived, were highly influential in the Progressive Era.

   a. Frederick Winslow Taylor
   b. Douglas N. Daft
   c. Jonah Jacob Goldberg
   d. Geoffrey Colvin

9. _____ has been described as the 'process of social influence in which one person can enlist the aid and support of others in the accomplishment of a common task' . A definition more inclusive of followers comes from Alan Keith of Genentech who said '_____ is ultimately about creating a way for people to contribute to making something extraordinary happen.'

_____ is one of the most salient aspects of the organizational context. However, defining _____ has been challenging.

   a. 28-hour day
   b. Situational leadership
   c. Leadership
   d. 1990 Clean Air Act

10. _____ is an advertisement in which a particular product specifically mentions a competitor by name for the express purpose of showing why the competitor is inferior to the product naming it.

This should not be confused with parody advertisements, where a fictional product is being advertised for the purpose of poking fun at the particular advertisement, nor should it be confused with the use of a coined brand name for the purpose of comparing the product without actually naming an actual competitor. ('Wikipedia tastes better and is less filling than the Encyclopedia Galactica.')

In the 1980s, during what has been referred to as the cola wars, soft-drink manufacturer Pepsi ran a series of advertisements where people, caught on hidden camera, in a blind taste test, chose Pepsi over rival Coca-Cola.

   a. 28-hour day
   b. 1990 Clean Air Act
   c. 33 Strategies of War
   d. Comparative advertising

Chapter 15. CHANGE LEADERSHIP AND STRESS

11. A _____ is a subset of the overall internal controls of a business covering the application of people, documents, technologies, and procedures by management accountants to solving business problems such as costing a product, service or a business-wide strategy. _____s are distinct from regular information systems in that they are used to analyze other information systems applied in operational activities in the organization. Academically, the term is commonly used to refer to the group of information management methods tied to the automation or support of human decision making, e.g. Decision Support Systems, Expert systems, and Executive information systems.

   a. 28-hour day
   b. Management information system
   c. Strategic information system
   d. 1990 Clean Air Act

12. _____. The objective of OD is to improve the organization's capacity to handle its internal and external functioning and relationships. This would include such things as improved interpersonal and group processes, more effective communication, enhanced ability to cope with organizational problems of all kinds, more effective decision processes, more appropriate leadership style, improved skill in dealing with destructive conflict, and higher levels of trust and cooperation among organizational members.

   a. Improved Organizational Performance
   b. Organizational structure
   c. Industrial relations
   d. Organizational development

13. Procter is a surname, and may also refer to:

   - Bryan Waller Procter (pseud. Barry Cornwall), English poet
   - Goodwin Procter, American law firm
   - _____, consumer products multinational

   a. Downstream
   b. Strict liability
   c. Procter ' Gamble
   d. Master and Servant Acts

14. _____ is a process of agreeing upon objectives within an organization so that management and employees agree to the objectives and understand what they are in the organization.

The term '_____' was first popularized by Peter Drucker in his 1954 book 'The Practice of Management'.

The essence of _____ is participative goal setting, choosing course of actions and decision making.

Chapter 15. CHANGE LEADERSHIP AND STRESS

   a. Business economics
   b. Job enrichment
   c. Clean sheet review
   d. Management by objectives

15. _____ is a term defined by the Oxford English Dictionary as an individual's 'course or progress through life '. It is usually considered to pertain to remunerative work (and sometimes also formal education.)

The etymology of the term is somewhat ironic in that it comes from the Latin word carrera, which means race .

   a. Career
   b. Spatial mismatch
   c. Career planning
   d. Nursing shortage

16. The _____ is a monograph published by Frederick Winslow Taylor in 1911. This influential monograph is the basis of modern organization and decision theory and has motivated administrators and students of managerial technique. Taylor was an American mechanical engineer and a management consultant in his later years.
   a. 1990 Clean Air Act
   b. 28-hour day
   c. 33 Strategies of War
   d. Principles of Scientific Management

17. _____ is a theory of management that analyzes and synthesizes workflows, with the objective of improving labour productivity. The core ideas of the theory were developed by Frederick Winslow Taylor in the 1880s and 1890s, and were first published in his monographs, Shop Management and The Principles of _____ Taylor believed that decisions based upon tradition and rules of thumb should be replaced by precise procedures developed after careful study of an individual at work.
   a. Master production schedule
   b. Value engineering
   c. Capacity planning
   d. Scientific Management

18. _____ Movement refers to those researchers of organizational development who study the behavior of people in groups, in particular workplace groups. It originated in the 1920s' Hawthorne studies, which examined the effects of social relations, motivation and employee satisfaction on factory productivity. The movement viewed workers in terms of their psychology and fit with companies, rather than as interchangeable parts.

Chapter 15. CHANGE LEADERSHIP AND STRESS

a. Hersey-Blanchard situational theory
b. Participatory management
c. Work design
d. Human relations

19. _____ refers to those researchers of organizational development who study the behavior of people in groups, in particular workplace groups. It originated in the 1920s' Hawthorne studies, which examined the effects of social relations, motivation and employee satisfaction on factory productivity. The movement viewed workers in terms of their psychology and fit with companies, rather than as interchangeable parts.
   a. Job satisfaction
   b. Path-goal theory
   c. Human relations movement
   d. Job analysis

20. The U.S. _____ is an independent agency of the United States government which holds primary responsibility for enforcing the federal securities laws and regulating the securities industry, the nation's stock and options exchanges, and other electronic securities markets. The SEC was created by section 4 of the Securities Exchange Act of 1934 (now codified as 15 U.S.C. Â§ 78d and commonly referred to as the 1934 Act.)
   a. 28-hour day
   b. 33 Strategies of War
   c. 1990 Clean Air Act
   d. Securities and Exchange Commission

21. _____ and Theory Y are theories of human motivation created and developed by Douglas McGregor at the MIT Sloan School of Management in the 1960s that have been used in human resource management, organizational behavior, organizational communication and organizational development. They describe two very different attitudes toward workforce motivation. McGregor felt that companies followed either one or the other approach.

In _____, which many managers practice, management assumes employees are inherently lazy and will avoid work if they can. They inherently dislike work. Because of this, workers need to be closely supervised and comprehensive systems of controls developed.

   a. Cash cow
   b. Management team
   c. Job enrichment
   d. Theory X

Chapter 15. CHANGE LEADERSHIP AND STRESS

22. Theory X and _____ are theories of human motivation created and developed by Douglas McGregor at the MIT Sloan School of Management in the 1960s that have been used in human resource management, organizational behavior, organizational communication and organizational development. They describe two very different attitudes toward workforce motivation. McGregor felt that companies followed either one or the other approach.

In _____, management assumes employees may be ambitious and self-motivated and exercise self-control. It is believed that employees enjoy their mental and physical work duties.

a. Design leadership
b. Business Workflow Analysis
c. Contingency theory
d. Theory Y

23. _____ of the learning curve effect and the closely related experience curve effect express the relationship between equations for experience and efficiency or between efficiency gains and investment in the effort. The experience of 'learning curves' was first observed by the 19th Century German psychologist Hermann Ebbinghaus according to the difficulty of memorizing varying numbers of verbal stimuli, and subsequent learning about the complex processes of learning are discussed in the

The rule used for representing the learning curve effect states that the more times a task has been performed, the less time will be required on each subsequent iteration.

a. Models
b. Spatial Decision Support Systems
c. Point biserial correlation coefficient
d. Distribution

24. _____ is a broad label that refers to any individuals or households that use goods and services generated within the economy. The concept of a _____ is used in different contexts, so that the usage and significance of the term may vary.

Typically when business people and economists talk of _____s they are talking about person as _____, an aggregated commodity item with little individuality other than that expressed in the buy/not-buy decision.

a. 1990 Clean Air Act
b. Consumer
c. 33 Strategies of War
d. 28-hour day

25. The _____ was enacted in 1972 by the United States Congress. It established the United States Consumer Product Safety Commission as an independent agency of the United States federal government and defined its basic authority. The act gives CPSC the power to develop safety standards and pursue recalls for products that present unreasonable or substantial risks of injury or death to consumers.
   a. Consumer Product Safety Act
   b. 1990 Clean Air Act
   c. 33 Strategies of War
   d. 28-hour day

26. _____ is a strategic planning method used to evaluate the Strengths, Weaknesses, Opportunities, and Threats involved in a project or in a business venture. It involves specifying the objective of the business venture or project and identifying the internal and external factors that are favorable and unfavorable to achieving that objective. The technique is credited to Albert Humphrey, who led a convention at Stanford University in the 1960s and 1970s using data from Fortune 500 companies.
   a. Corporate image
   b. Marketing
   c. Market share
   d. SWOT analysis

27. _____ is any process of estimating or inferring how local policies, actions, or changes influences the state of the neighboring universe. It also can be defined, as an approach to problem solving, as viewing 'problems' as parts of an overall system, rather than reacting to present outcomes or events and potentially contributing to further development of the undesired issue or problem. _____ is a framework that is based on the belief that the component parts of a system can best be understood in the context of relationships with each other and with other systems, rather than in isolation.
   a. 28-hour day
   b. 1990 Clean Air Act
   c. Systems theory
   d. Systems thinking

Chapter 1
1. d	2. a	3. d	4. a	5. d	6. d	7. d	8. a	9. d	10. a
11. d	12. c	13. b	14. c	15. d	16. c	17. c	18. d	19. d	20. d
21. b	22. a	23. d	24. c	25. d	26. c	27. b	28. d	29. d	30. d
31. d									

Chapter 2
1. d	2. d	3. d	4. d	5. a	6. d	7. c	8. c	9. a	10. c
11. b	12. d	13. d	14. b	15. d	16. b	17. d	18. b	19. d	20. d
21. a	22. a	23. d	24. c	25. a	26. c				

Chapter 3
1. d	2. a	3. d	4. c	5. c	6. b	7. a	8. c	9. d	10. d
11. a	12. b	13. d	14. d	15. d	16. d	17. b	18. d	19. c	20. d
21. d	22. a	23. d	24. d						

Chapter 4
1. d	2. c	3. c	4. b	5. a	6. d	7. c	8. d	9. a	10. b
11. a	12. d	13. d	14. a	15. d	16. d	17. a	18. d	19. d	

Chapter 5
1. d	2. d	3. b	4. d	5. b	6. d	7. b	8. d	9. b	10. b
11. b	12. d	13. d	14. d	15. d	16. b	17. d	18. d	19. d	20. d
21. c	22. c								

Chapter 6
1. a	2. b	3. d	4. d	5. a	6. d	7. d	8. d	9. d	10. b
11. d	12. d	13. b	14. c	15. d	16. a	17. a	18. d	19. d	20. b
21. d	22. d	23. b	24. b	25. d	26. d	27. b	28. d	29. d	30. d
31. d	32. c								

Chapter 7
1. d	2. d	3. b	4. d	5. b	6. a	7. a	8. a	9. b	10. b
11. d	12. d	13. d	14. d	15. d	16. d	17. c	18. c	19. d	20. d
21. d	22. d								

Chapter 8
1. d	2. d	3. d	4. b	5. d	6. d	7. d	8. d	9. d	10. a
11. a	12. a	13. b	14. d	15. d	16. d				

Chapter 9
1. b	2. d	3. d	4. d	5. b	6. d	7. c	8. d	9. d	10. d
11. c	12. d	13. b							

ANSWER KEY

Chapter 10
1. d 2. c 3. d 4. d 5. d 6. c 7. d 8. d 9. d 10. b
11. d 12. d 13. d 14. d 15. a 16. d 17. b 18. d 19. d 20. a
21. d 22. d 23. d 24. a 25. d 26. a 27. a 28. c 29. b 30. d
31. d 32. d 33. d 34. d 35. b 36. a 37. d

Chapter 11
1. b 2. a 3. a 4. a 5. b 6. d 7. a 8. c

Chapter 12
1. d 2. d 3. d 4. c 5. b 6. d 7. c 8. d 9. d 10. d
11. d 12. d 13. d 14. d 15. d 16. d 17. d 18. b 19. a 20. b
21. b 22. d 23. d 24. d 25. b 26. b 27. c 28. d 29. a 30. d
31. d 32. d 33. c 34. a 35. d 36. b 37. a 38. c

Chapter 13
1. d 2. b 3. c 4. c 5. a 6. a 7. b 8. d 9. b 10. c
11. c 12. a 13. d

Chapter 14
1. a 2. d 3. d 4. d 5. d 6. d 7. a 8. d 9. c 10. a
11. d 12. b 13. d 14. d 15. d

Chapter 15
1. b 2. d 3. d 4. b 5. d 6. a 7. d 8. a 9. c 10. d
11. b 12. a 13. c 14. d 15. a 16. d 17. d 18. d 19. c 20. d
21. d 22. d 23. a 24. b 25. a 26. d 27. d